Zimbabwe, Botswana & Namibia

a Lonely Planet travel atlas

Zimbabwe, Botswana & Namibia - travel atlas

1st edition

Published by
Lonely Planet Publications
Head Office: PO Box 617, Hawthorn, Vic 3122, Australia
Branches: 155 Filbert St, Suite 251, Oakland, CA 94607, USA
                   10 Barley Mow Passage, Chiswick, London W4 4PH, UK
                   71 bis rue du Cardinal Lemoine, 75005 Paris, France

Cartography by
Steinhart Katzir Publishers Ltd
Fax: 972-3-696 1360

Printed by
Colorcraft Ltd, Hong Kong

Photographs by
Chris Barton, Alex Dissanayake, Peter Ptschelinzew, Deanna Swaney,
David Wall

Front cover: Elephants, Okavango Delta, Botswana (David Wall)
Back cover:: Cheetah, Hwange National Park, Zimbabwe (Alex Dissanayake)
Title page: Gemsbok (Oryx), Namib-Naukluft National Park, Namibia (David Wall)

First Published
January 1996

Although the authors and publisher have tried to make the information as accurate as possible, they accept no responsibility for any loss, injury or inconvenience sustained by any person using this book.

National Library of Australia Cataloguing in Publication Data

Swaney, Deanna
    Zimbabwe, Botswana and Namibia travel atlas.

    1st ed.
    Includes index.
    ISBN 0 86442 274 1.

    1. Botswana - Road maps. 2. Botswana - Maps, Tourist.
    3. Namibia - Road maps. 4. Namibia - Maps, Tourist.
    5. Zimbabwe - Road maps. 6. Zimbabwe - Maps, Tourist.
    I. Swaney, Deanna. (Series : Lonely Planet travel atlas).

912.688

Contents

Deanna Swaney

After completing university studies, Deanna Swaney made a shoe-string tour of Europe and has been addicted to travel ever since. Despite an erstwhile career in computer programming, she managed intermittent forays away from encroaching yuppiedom in midtown Anchorage, Alaska, and at first opportunity, made a break for South America where she wrote Lonely Planet's *Bolivia – a travel survival kit*. Subsequent travels led through an erratic circuit of island paradises – Arctic and tropical – and resulted in three more travel survival kits: *Tonga*, *Samoa* and *Iceland, Greenland & the Faroe Islands*.

The author of the Lonely Planet guide to *Zimbabwe, Botswana & Namibia*, Deanna was the obvious choice to research the *Zimbabwe, Botswana & Namibia* travel atlas. Deanna has also worked on Lonely Planet guides to *Brazil*, *Madagascar & Comoros* and *Mauritius, Réunion & Seychelles*, as well as contributing to Shoestring guides to Africa, South America and Scandinavia.

About this Atlas

This book is another addition to the Lonely Planet travel atlas series. Designed to tie in with the equivalent Lonely Planet guidebook, we hope the *Zimbabwe, Botswana & Namibia* travel atlas helps travellers enjoy their trip even more. As well as detailed, accurate maps, this atlas also contains a multi-lingual map legend, useful travel information in five languages, and a comprehensive index to ensure easy location-finding.

The maps were checked out by Deanna Swaney as part of her preparation for a new edition of Lonely Planet's *Zimbabwe, Botswana & Namibia* guidebook.

From the Publishers

Thanks to Danny Schapiro, chief cartographer at Steinhart Katzir Publishers, who researched and drew the maps with the assistance of Galit Shiran, and also to Mira Rotholtz who prepared the index. At Lonely Planet, the mapping was checked by Paul Smitz, Michelle Stamp and Lou Byrnes, who also edited the index. Layout, design and cover design was completed by David Kemp. Thanks also to Claire Minty and Susan Noonan for their help.

The language sections were coordinated with the assistance of Yoshiharu Abe, Pedro Diaz, Megan Fraser, Christine Gruettke, Sergio Mariscal, Isabelle Muller and Penelope Richardson.

Request

This atlas is designed to be clear, comprehensive and reliable. We hope you'll find it a worthy addition to your Lonely Planet travel library. Even if you don't, please let us know! All suggestions and corrections are welcome – write to Lonely Planet and tell us what you think.

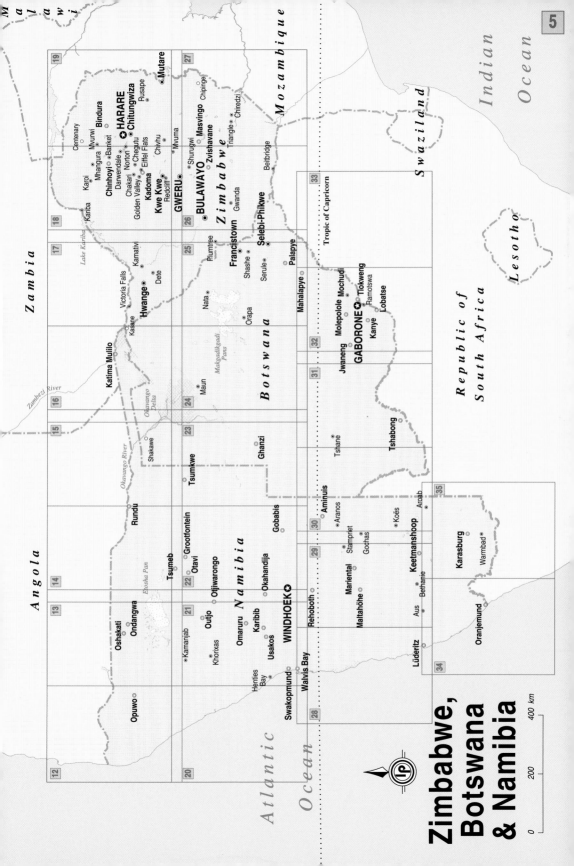

Zimbabwe,
Botswana
& Namibia

*Epupa
Falls*

*Ondorusu
Falls*

*Ruacana
Falls*

Opuwo C41

Atlantic

Ocean

*Skeleton Coast
Park Wilderness*

Terrace Bay

Torra Bay C39

*Twyfelfonte
Rock Engrav*

*National West Coast
Recreation Area*

*Cape Cross
Seal Reserve*

Tropic of Capricorn
· ·

Namibia &
Western Botswana

0   100   200 km

	Highway
	Regional Road
----	Railway

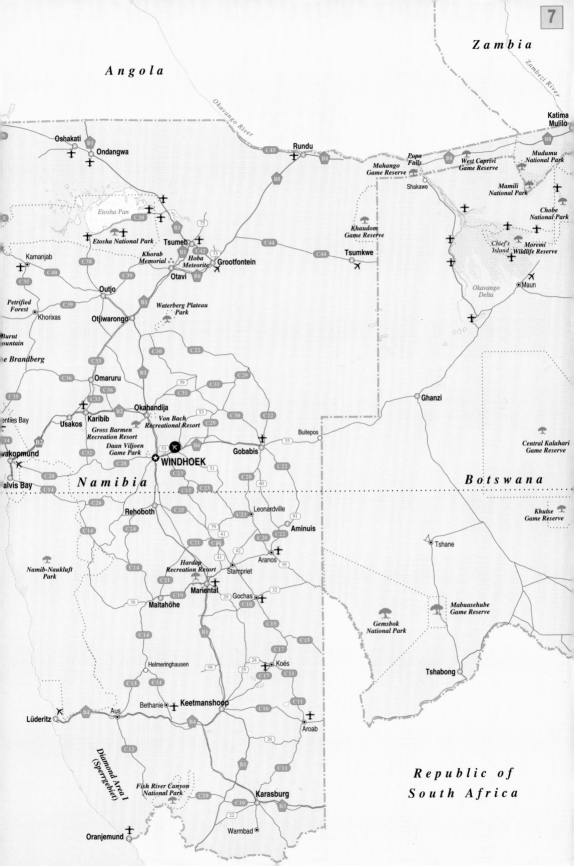

Z a m b i a

A n g o l a

Zambezi River

Okavango River

5

Oshakati

B1 Ondangwa

Katima Mulilo

B8

C45 Rundu

B8

Popa Falls B8 West Caprivi Game Reserve Mudumu National Park

B8

Mahango Game Reserve

Shakawe

Mamili National Park

Etosha Pan

C38

Khaudom Game Reserve

Chobe National Park

Etosha National Park

Tsumeb

C44

C44 Tsumkwe

Chief's Island Moremi Wildlife Reserve

Kamanjab

C38

B1 C42 73

Hoba Meteorite Grootfontein

Okavango Delta

Maun

C35 C40

Khorab Memorial

75

C35 C39 Otavi B8

C39

Petrified Forest

Outjo

Khorixas

C39

Waterberg Plateau Park

B1

Ghanzi

Burnt Mountain

C36

Otjiwarongo

the Brandberg

C33

C30 C22

Central Kalahari Game Reserve

C36 Omaruru

59

C35 C33 B2

C31 C29

Karibib

Okahandija 53

Buitepos

Usakos

Gross Barmen Recreation Resort Von Bach Recreational Resort C30 C22

enties Bay

C32 Daan Viljoen Game Park 53 B6 Gobabis 55

34 B2

C28 WINDHOEK

Khutse Game Reserve

wakopmund

51

B o t s w a n a

alvis Bay C28 C14

N a m i b i a

C23 C20 40

Tshane

C26 C15 C23

Rehoboth C25

C23 Leonardville 91

C14 C24 79 C20 C22 Aminuis

C21 C15 41 42 39

C14 Hardap Recreation Resort 41 Aranos

Namib-Naukluft Park C21 Stampriet Mabuasehube Game Reserve

36 C19 Mariental Gochas 32

Maltahöhe 29 C18

Gemsbok National Park

C14 C15

B1 C17 C15

Helmeringhausen 98 24 Koës

C14 C13 29 C17 C11

Tshabong

C13 C14 C16 C11

Bethanie Keetmanshoop

Lüderitz B4 Aus B4 Aroab

C13 26

Diamond Area 1 (Sperrgebiet) B1

Fish River Canyon National Park C10 C11

R e p u b l i c   o f
S o u t h   A f r i c a

C10 B3 Karasburg

22

Oranjemund Warmbad

Z a m b i a

A n g o l a

Zambezi River

Mana Pools
National Park

Hurungwe
Safari Area

A1

Kariba

Kuburi Wilderness Area

Charara
Safari Area

Lake Kariba

Lake Kariba
Recreational Park

Matusadona
National Park

Chete
Safari Area

Katima Mulilo

B8

Okavango River

Rundu

B8

Popa
Falls

B8

Mahango
Game Reserve

West Caprivi
Game Reserve

Mudumu
National Park

Shakawe

Mamili
National Park

Chobe
Forest Reserve

Kasane
Forest Reserve

Matetsi
Safari
Area

Zambezi
N.P.
Victoria Falls

Sijarira
Forest Area

Chirisa
Safari Area

Chizarira
National Park

Hartley
Safari A

Kamativi

Khaudom
Game Reserve

Chobe
National Park

Maikaelelo
Forest Reserve

Panda-Masuie Forest Land
Kazuma Pan N.P.

Kazuma Kazuma Forest Land
Forest Reserve

Hwange

A8

Mzolo Forest
Reserve

Ngamo
Forest Land

Lake Alice
Forest Land

Z i m b a b w

Tsumkwe

C44

Chief's
Island

Moremi
Wildlife Reserve

Matetsi Safari
Area

Deka Safari Area

Dete

Sibuyu
Forest Reserve

Hwange
National Park

Gwaai
Forest Land

Inseze
Forest Land

Nalat
Ruir

N a m i b i a

*Okavango
Delta*

Maun

Makgadikgadi
& Nxai Pan
National Park

Nata

Chesa
Forest Land

Bila Ruins
Danangombe
Ruins

Zinjanja
Ruins

BULAWAYO

Plumtree

Lake Cunningh
Recreational Pa

Ghanzi

B o t s w a n a

*Makgadikgadi
Pans*

Matobo
National Park

Gwanda

Central Kalahari
Game Reserve

Orapa

Shashe

Francistown

Serule

Selebi-Phikwe

Tuli Safa
Area

North-East T
Game Reser

Serowe

Palapye

Tuli Block Farms

Khutse
Game Reserve

Mahalapye

39

Tshane

Molepolole

Mochudi

Jwaneng

GABORONE

Tlokweng

Mabuasehube
Game Reserve

Kanye

Kanye
Ruins

Ramotswa

Gemsbok
National Park

Lobatse

C15

Ramathlabama

Tshabong

Malopo River

*R e p u b l i c   o f
S o u t h   A f r i c a*

Aroab

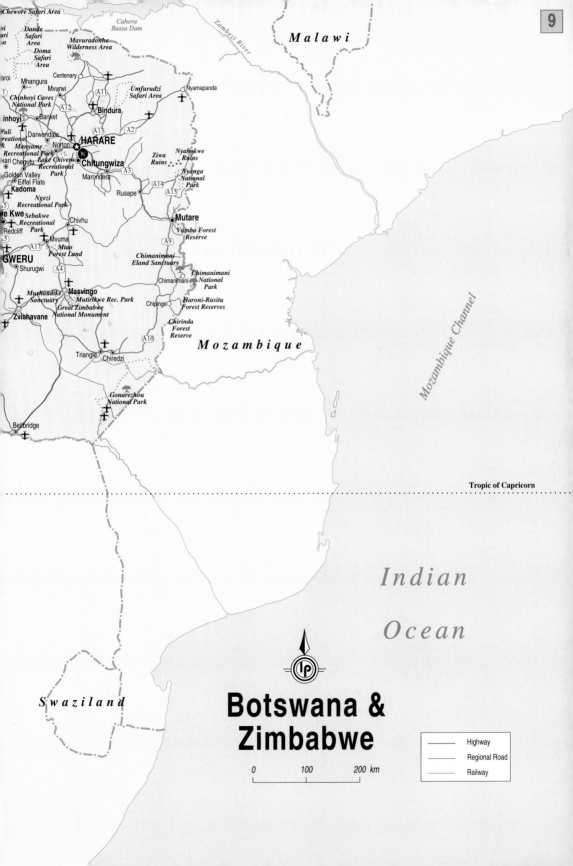

Chewore Safari Area

Dande Safari Area

Mavuradonha Wilderness Area

Doma Safari Area

Cahora Bassa Dam

Zambezi River

M a l a w i

Centenary

Mhangura
Mvurwi
Chinhoyi Caves National Park
Banket
A11
A12
Bindura
A13
Darwendale
Norton
HARARE
Chitungwiza
A2

Umfurudzi Safari Area
Nyamapanda

inhoyi

uli
reational
Manyame Recreational Park
Lake Chivero Recreational Park
kari
Chegutu
Golden Valley
Eiffel Flats
Kadoma
Ngezi Recreational Park
Marondera
A3
Rusape
A14
A15

Ziwa Ruins
Nyahokwe Ruins
Nyanga National Park

e Kwe
Sebakwe Recreational Park
Redcliff
A17
Mvuma
Mtao Forest Land
Chivhu

GWERU
Shurugwi
A4

Mushandike Sanctuary
Masvingo
Mutirikwe Rec. Park
Great Zimbabwe National Monument
Zvishavane
Chipinge
Chimanimani Eland Sanctuary
Chimanimani
Chimanimani National Park
Haroni-Rusitu Forest Reserves

Mutare
Vumba Forest Reserve
A9

Chirinda Forest Reserve

Triangle
A10
Chiredzi

M o z a m b i q u e

Gonarezhou National Park

Beitbridge

Mozambique Channel

Tropic of Capricorn

I n d i a n

O c e a n

S w a z i l a n d

Botswana &
Zimbabwe

———	Highway
———	Regional Road
·········	Railway

0   100   200 km

MAP LEGEND

HARARE City

Kwe Kwe ◉ Major Town

Bindura ◎ Town

Chegutu ◉ Small Town

Sherwood ○ Village

WINDHOEK Capital City
Capitale
Hauptstadt
Capital
首都

★ Capital City (Locator map)
Capitale (Carte de situation)
Hauptstadt (Orientierungskarte)
Capital (Mapa Localizador)
首都(地図上の位置)

International Boundary
Limites Internationales
Staatsgrenze
Frontera Internacional
国境

District Boundary
Limites du District
Bezirksgrenze
Límite de Distrito
地区の境界

Major Highway
Route Nationale
Femstraße
Carretera Principal
主要な国道

Highway
Route Principale
Landstraße
Carretera
国道

Regional Road
Route Régionale
Regionale Fernstraße
Carretera Regional
地方道

Secondary Road
Route Secondaire
Nebenstraße
Carretera Secundaria
二級道路

Minor Road
Route Secondaire
Nebenstraße
Carretera Secundaria
小道

Railway
Voie de chemin de fer
Eisenbahn
Ferrocarril
鉄道

Mapunga
Railway station
Gare Ferroviaire
Bahnhof
Estación de Ferrocarril
駅

Route Number (Major Highway)
Numérotation Routière
Routenummer
Ruta Número
道路の番号(主要な国道)

4 B1 Route Number (Highway)
Numérotation Routière
Routenummer
Ruta Número
道路の番号(国道)

C41 B1 Route Number (Regional Road)
Numérotation Routière
Routenummer
Ruta Número
道路の番号(地方道)

D3612 Route Number (Secondary Road)
Numérotation Routière
Routenummer
Ruta Número
道路の番号(二級道路)

40 Distance in Kilometres
Distance en Kilomètres
Entfernung in Kilometern
Distancia en Kilómetros
距離（km）

✈ International Airport
Aéroport International
Internationaler Flughafen
Aeropuerto Internacional
国際空港

✈ Domestic Airport
Aéroport National
Inlandflughafen
Aeropuerto Interior
国内線空港

✈	**Airfield** Aérodrome Flugplatz Pista de Aterrizaje 飛行機発着場	*Groot Tirasberg* *1867* ⊹	**Mountain** Montagne Berg Montaña 山	**Pan** Marasi Salant Salzmulde Cuenca Salobreña 窪地
✝	**Church** Église Kirche Iglesia 教会	*II*	**Pass** Col Paß Desfiladero 峠	**Tropics** Tropiques Tropen Los Trópicos 回帰線
	Castle/Fort Château/Château Fort Burg/Festung Castillo/Fuerte 城・砦		**National Park/ Game Reserve** Parc National/Réserve Nationalpark/Wildreservat Parque Nacional/Reserva de Fauna 国立公園・動物保護地域	
⛽	**Petrol Station** Station-Service Tankstelle Gasolinera ガソリンスタンド		**Forest Reserve/Safari Area** Réserve Forestière/Zone de Safari Geschütztes/Safarigebiet Reserva Forestal/Area de Safari 森林保護地域・サファリ区	
∴	**Ruins** Ruines Ruinen Ruinas 遺跡	～	**River** Fleuve/Rivière Fluß Río 川	
※	**Viewpoint** Point de Vue Aussicht Mirador 展望地点		**Lake** Lac See Lago 湖	
▲	**Camping Ground** Terrain de Camping Zeltplatz Camping キャンプ場	∘⌐	**Spring** Source Quelle Manantial 泉	
⌂	**Lighthouse** Phare Leuchtturm Faro 灯台		**Waterfall** Cascades Wasserfall Cascada 滝	
	Seaport Port de Mer Seehafen Puerto Marítimo 港		**Desert** Désert Wüste Desierto 砂漠	
	Beach Plage Strand Playa 海岸		**Swamp** Marais Sumpf Pantano 沼地	
	Cave Grotte Höhle Cueva 洞窟			

3500 m
3000 m
2500 m
2000 m
1500 m
1000 m
500 m
200 m
100 m
0
-150 m
-300 m
-900 m
-3000 m

0   20   40   60   80   100 km

1 : 2 000 000

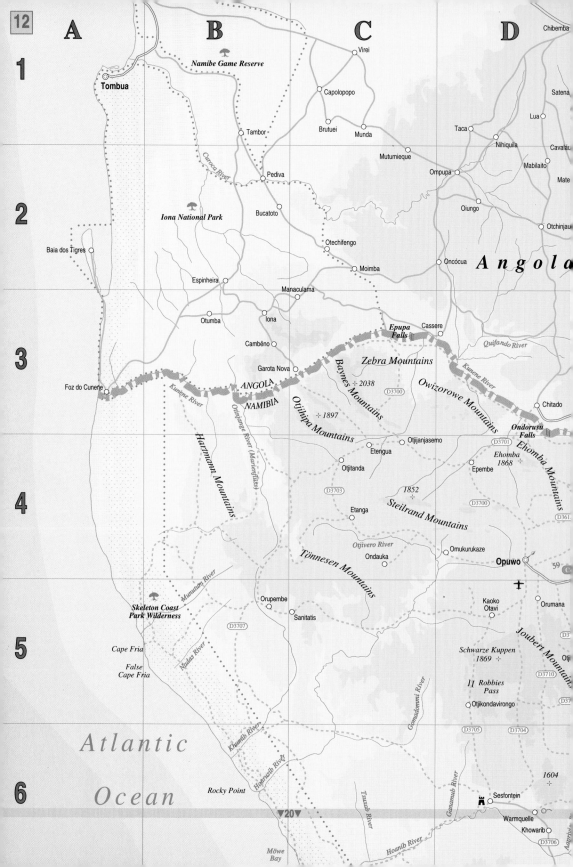

A   **B**   **C**   **D**

1

Tombua

Namibe Game Reserve

Virei

Capolopopo

Brutuei   Munda

Tambor

Mutumieque

Taca

Satena

Lua

Nihiquila

Cavalău

Mabilaito

Mate

2

Pediva

Ompupa

Otchinjau

Iona National Park

Bucatoto

Oiungo

Baia dos Tigres

Otechifengo

Moimba

Oncócua

A n g o l a

Espinheira

Manaculama

3

Otumba

Iona

Cambêno

Garota Nova

Epupa
Falls

Cassere

Quifando River

Zebra Mountains

Baynes Mountains

Kunene River

Chitado

ANGOLA

÷ 2038

D3700

Owizorowe Mountains

NAMIBIA

Foz do Cunene

Kunene River

Otjihipa Mountains

÷ 1897

Ondorusu
Falls

4

Hartmann Mountains

Otjinjange River (Marienfluss)

Otjijanjasemo

D3701

Ehomba
1868 ÷

Ehomba Mountains

Etengua

Otjitanda

D3703

1852
÷

Epembe

D3700

D361

Etanga

Steilrand Mountains

Otjivero River

Omukurukaze

Opuwo

59

Ondauka

Tönnesen Mountains

✛

5

Skeleton Coast
Park Wilderness

Orupembe

Sanitatis

D3707

Kaoko
Otavi

Orumana

Cape Fria

Nadas River

Schwarze Kuppen
1869 ÷

Joubert Mountains

Otji

D3710

False
Cape Fria

Robbies
Pass

D37

Otjikondavirongo

6

Atlantic

Khumib River

Hoarusib River

Gomadommi River

1604
÷

Ocean

Rocky Point

Tsuxab River

Sesfontein

Ganumub River

Warmquelle

▼20▼

Hoanib River

Khowarib

D3706

Möwe
Bay

14

A | B | C | D

1

Caiundo
Baixo Longa
Cuito River

2

Salonga
Chimbueta
Cucio River
Mucundi
Candelela
Tunga
Cuatir River
Longa River
Nankova
Rito
Utembo River
Nheha River

3

Savate
Catambué
Okavango River
Deleto
Chissombo River
Matende
Sandála
Cauno
Maué
Macai
Samugalengue
Mavengue
Cafuma River
Caqueue River

ANGOLA
NAMIBIA

Capasso
Mingoje
Cuangar
Cudumo
D3405

▼13▼
D3601
Okongo
D3601
Oshifutu
Ekoka
D3603
Nkurenkuru
D3407
Mpungu
D3404
Nepara
Dala
Tondoro
Sessua
Canjime
Bengo
Mica
Dango
119
Lupala
C45
Sambusu
Mupini
Runc
Mpuku River

4

Namungundo River
Tsitsib

5

Omuthiya River
199
B8

Namibia

Operet
Fischer's Pan
Oshivelo
Mangetti
Adom River
Namutoni
Von Lindequist Gate
Mokuti
C38
B1
D3001
D3004
Owambo River
Tsintsabis
D3016
D3016
Karakuwis
D3028
81
D3047
D2908
D3007
D2855
D2848
D2848

6

🌳 **Etosha National Park**
D3025
D3017
D2862
Maroelaboom
D2898
72
75
▼22▼
C44
Kano Vlei
Guinas
D3028
D3043
Otjikoto
56
Abenab
32
D2868
D2893
Omatako Riv
Lake Otjikoto
92
D2845
Tsumeb
Bobos
B1
C42
Lake Guinas
D2866
34

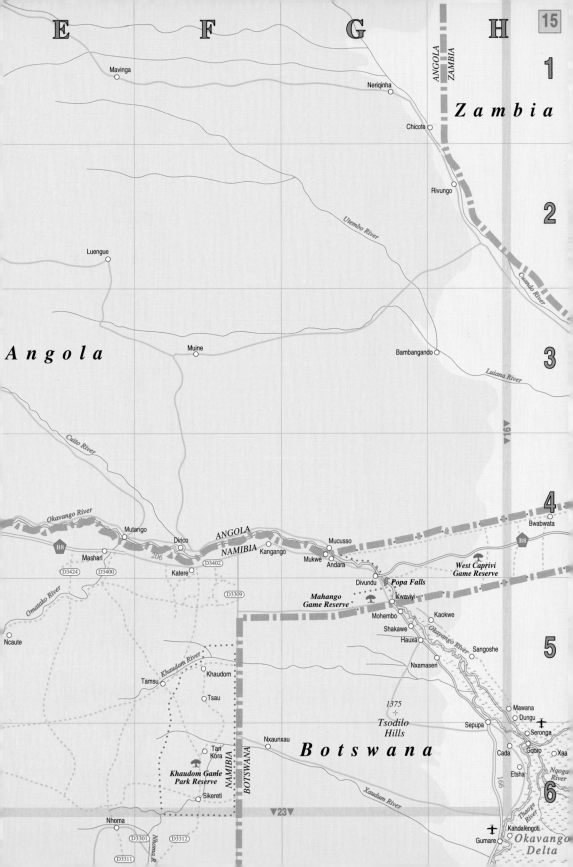

1

2

3

4

5

6

Mavinga

Neriqinha

Chicote

Z a m b i a

ANGOLA
ZAMBIA

Rivungo

Utembo River

Luengue

Cuando River

A n g o l a

Muine

Bambangando

Luiana River

Cuito River

16

Okavango River

Mutango

Dirico

ANGOLA

Mucusso

Bwabwata

B8

Mashari

206

Katere

NAMIBIA

Kangango

Mukwe

Andara

D3402

*West Caprivi
Game Reserve*

B8

D3424 D3400

Divundu Popa Falls

*Mahango
Game Reserve*

Kwaviyi

Ncaute

D3309

Mohembo

Kaokwe

Shakawe

Hauxa

Sangoshe

Okavango River

5

Khaudom River

Tamsu

Khaudom

Nxamaseri

1375

Mawana

Dungu

Tsau

*Tsodilo
Hills*

Sepupa

Seronga

Tari
Kora

Nxaunxau

B o t s w a n a

Cada

Gqoro Xaa

*Khaudom Game
Park Reserve*

NAMIBIA

BOTSWANA

Etsha

*Ngoga
River*

Sikereti

166

23

Nhoma

Xaudum River

*Thaoge
River*

6

D3301 D3312

Nhoma R.

Kandalengoti

D3311

Gumare *Okavango
Delta*

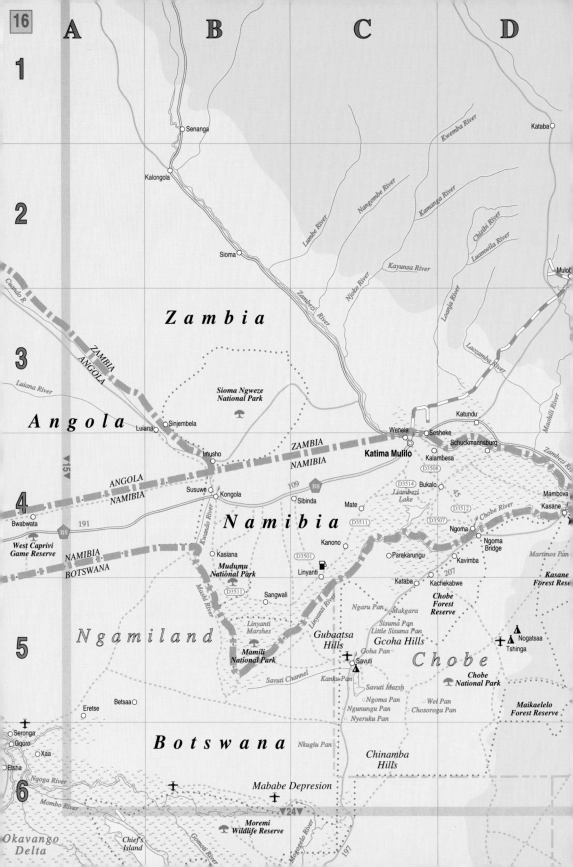

A **B** **C** **D**

1

2

3

4

5

6

Senanga

Kataba

Kalongola

Kwemba River

Nangombe River

Kamanga River

Chisibi River

Luanwila River

Sioma

Lambe River

Njoko River

Kayunsa River

Mulob

Cuando R.

Zambezi River

Loanja River

Laozamba River

Maohili River

Z a m b i a

ZAMBIA
ANGOLA

Luiana River

Sioma Ngweze
National Park

Katundu

Wenela

Sesheke

Schuckmannsburg

Zambezi Ri.

A n g o l a

Sinjembela

Luiana

Imusho

ZAMBIA
NAMIBIA

Katima Mulilo

Kalambesa

D3508

ANGOLA
NAMIBIA

Susuwe

Kongola

109

B8

Sibinda

Mate

*Liambezi
Lake*

D3514

Bukalo

45

Mambova

Kasane

▽15▽

Bwabwata

B8   191

Mashi River

N a m i b i a

Kanono

D3511

D3501

D3507

Ngoma

Chobe River

Ngoma
Bridge

D3512

NAMIBIA
BOTSWANA

West Capriri
Game Reserve

Kasiana

Mudumu
National Park

Linyanti

Parakarungu

Kavimba

Martinos Pan

**Kasane
Forest Rese**

207

D3511

Sangwali

Kwando River

Linyanti River

Kataba

Kachekabwe

**Chobe
Forest
Reserve**

N g a m i l a n d

*Linyanti
Marshes*

Mamili
National Park

Ngaru Pan

Makgara

Sisuma Pan
Little Sisuma Pan

Goha Pan

Savuti

Gubaatsa
Hills

Gcoha Hills

✞ Nogatsaa

Tshinga

C h o b e

Chobe
National Park

Savuti Channel

Kanku Pan

Savuti Marsh

**Maikaelelo
Forest Reserve**

Betsaa

Eretse

Seronga
Gqoro

Xaa

Etsha

Ngoma Pan

Ngunungu Pan

Nyeruku Pan

Wei Pan

Chosoroga Pan

B o t s w a n a

Nkugiu Pan

**Chinamba
Hills**

Ngoga River

Mombo River

Mababe Depresion

▽24▽

Gomoti River

Mogogelo River

197

**Okavango
Delta**

*Chief's
Island*

Moremi
Wildlife Reserve

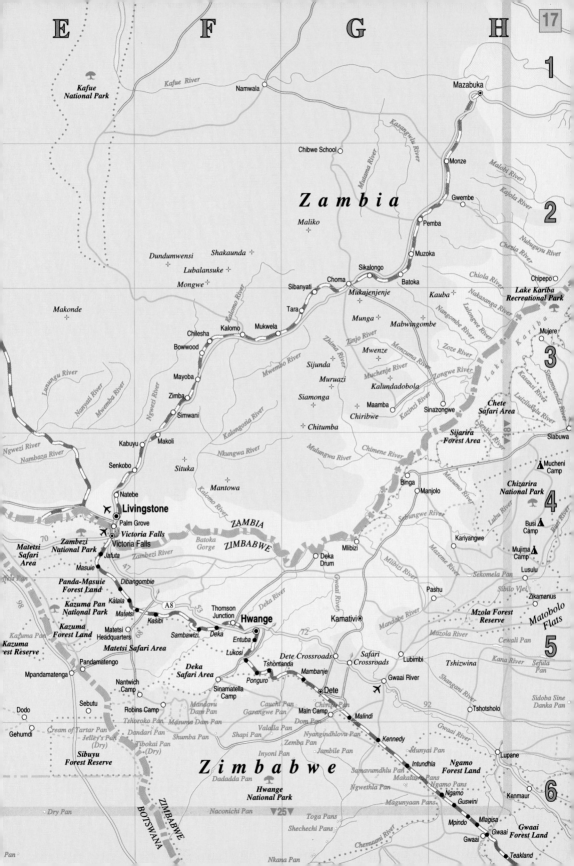

A   **B**   **C**   **D**

ZAMBIA · Zumbo
ZIMBABWE · Kanyemba · Panha

1

LUSAKA

Zambia

Kafue

Mbimbi

Chiawa
Nyamepi Camp

Zambezi River

Chewore Camp

Kafue River

Hurungwe
Safari Area

Chirundu

A1

Lusitu

Lusitu River

Taswe River

Mana Pools
National Park

Sapi
Safari
Area

Chewore
Safari
Area

−1245

Dande
Safari
Area

MOZAMBIQUE

Mushumbi
Pools

2

Nubuguyu River

Bungua

Kiora
Marongora
Rukomechi

Makuti
Myove

Gota Gota
Chipitani

Charara
Safari Area

Ramara
Chitanga

Manyangau
·1411

Manganyai

Ambakwe

Chidoma

Vuti

80

Doma
Safari
Area

Kariba

Kubiri
Wilderness Area

Sanyati
West Camp

Tashinga
Camp

Charara

Dandawa

Chararo River

Tsororo River

Kasigo River

Chivutsisigo

Wanyonzi

Nurige

Kalukumbula

Makore

Tangasa

Karoi

A1

Magugusi
·1367

Mwami

Chouka
Hills

Dopa

Mhangura

Silverside Mine

Raffingora

Mutorashan

Matusadona
National Park

Nyadara River

Kanyati River

Deve

Magunge

Madadzi

Manyame Range

Chipepo

Bumi Hills

Mujere

Lake Kariba
Recreational Park

Ume River

Zemaiwa

Zemaiwa

Birimahwe

Mapongola Hills

Matuzviadonha Range

Nyongwicha

Gachegache River

Chidamoye

Gwiwa

Tengwe

Zave

Chinhoyi Caves
National Park

Mezwikadet
Dam

3

Slabuwa

Manyabe Vlei

Matunga Shav

Gonde Vlei

Sengwa

Madziwadzido

Muma

Massimassu Pan

Mtirikati

Chimusimbe

Kawaya

Fletcher

Mutimrengwa

Zumbo
·1132

Biriwiri River

Sangwe

Lions Den

Alaska

Chinhoyi

24

Eldorado

Dunphaile

Banket

47

A1

Kildonan

Lembwe

Mping

Greycourt

Trelawney

Argo

Seki

Maryland

Gresham

4

Manzituba Vlei

Mucheni
Camp

Chizarira
National Park

Madziwadzido

Sipani Vlei

Busi River

Busi
Camp

Mujima
Camp

Chirisa Safari
Area

Tjibuli

Ntaba Mangwe

Kadoma

Gorodema

Chinyenyetsi

Hartley
Safari Area

Umfuli
Recreational
Park

Madakwe
·1123

Chakari

Mucheka Wa-Kla
Sunga Beta
Mountains

Murombedzi

Zwimba

Madzongwe

Gadzema

Selous

Darwendale

Lake
Manyame

Manyame
Recreational Park

Kutama

Makwiro

A5

Chibe

35

Selous

5

Lusulu

Zikamanus

Matobolo Flats

Malimasindi

Sengwa River

Mafungabusi
Plateau

Mbumbusi River

Gokwe

Njelele

Mafungabusi Peak
·1254

Nyampane Vlei

Golden
Valley

Chigwell

Martin

Chegutu

Duchess Hill

Mupfure River

Mat

Nyamwed

Lutope River

Mafungabusi
Forest Land

Empress
Mine

Rimuka

Eiffel Flats

Kadoma

Umsweswe

Umsweswe River

Manywe

Mashava Mountains

6

Sefula Pan

Sidoba Sine Danka Pan

Gwelutshina

Dagamella Pan

Dagamela

Gozho Pan

Lukampa

Tshwati Pan

Lupane River

Kenmaur

Lake Alice
Forest Land

Hlawe Pan

Nkayi

Zenko Pan

Silobela

Gwampa River

Gweru River

Zhombe

Jombe

Battlefields

Sherwood

Samwari

Lower Zivagwe Dam

Kwe Kwe

Gado

Redcliff

A5

Hunters Road

Umniati

39

Sebakwe River

Ngezi
Recreational
Park

Ngezi Dam

Mwinezi

Sebakwe Dam

Sebakwe
Recreational Park

Gobo

Lalapanzi

A17

Fairfield

Mvum

Gwaai
Forest Land

Ingiza River

Bubi River

Lungushi Pan

Tunke River

Vungu River

Shangani River

Maboleni

Insukummi

Zaloba

Connemara

Nahla

Sekope

61

Manyame

40

Quarry

Indiva

43

▼26▼

Zimbabwe

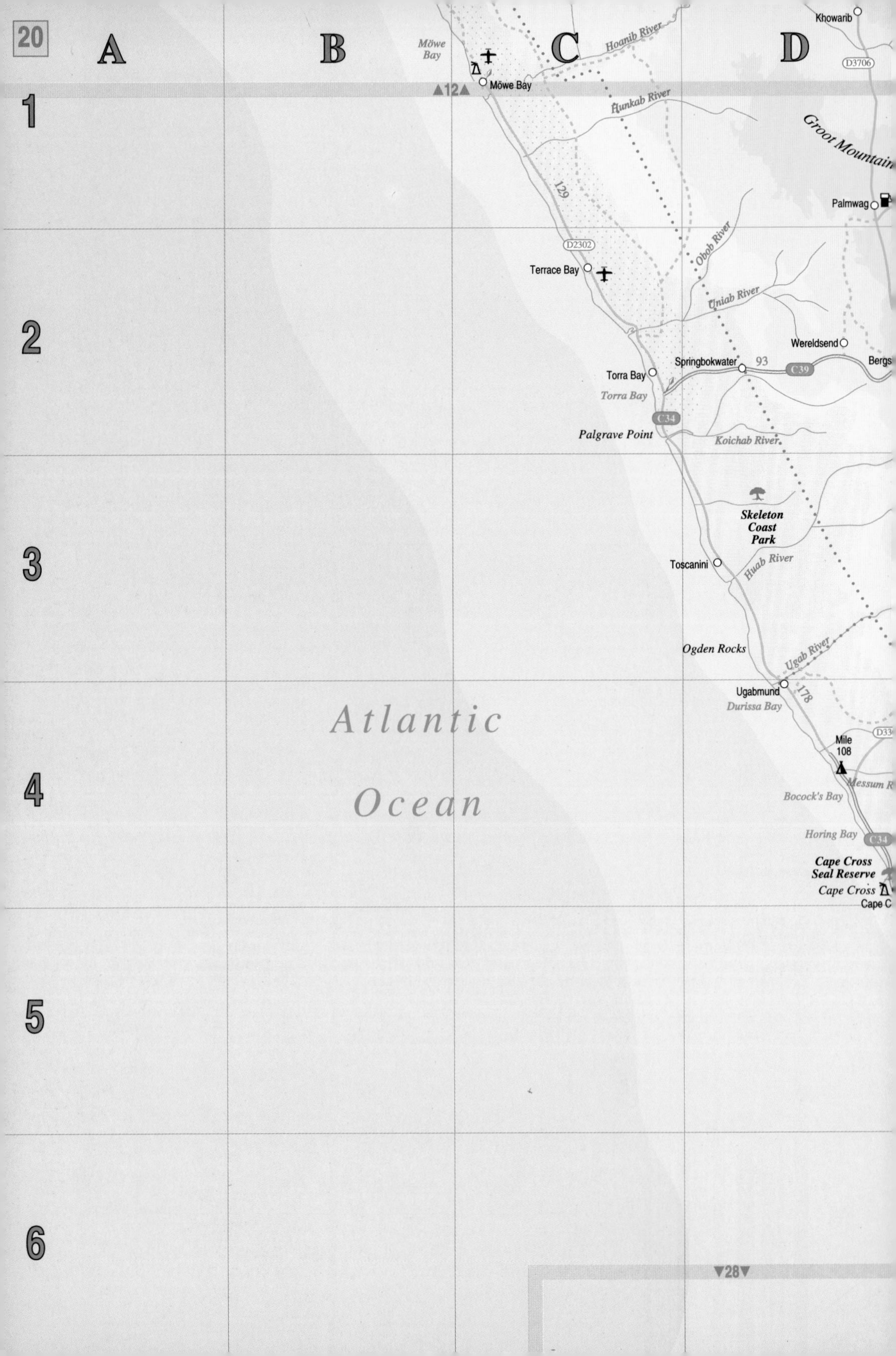

A B C D

1

2

3

4

5

6

Khowarib

Möwe
Bay

Hoanib River

Möwe Bay

▲12▲

Hunkab River

D3706

Groot Mountain

129

Palmwag

D2302

Obob River

Terrace Bay

Uniab River

Wereldsend

Springbokwater 93 C39 Bergs

Torra Bay

Torra Bay

C34

Palgrave Point

Koichab River

Skeleton
Coast
Park

Toscanini

Huab River

Ogden Rocks

Ugab River

Ugabmund 178

Durissa Bay

D33

Atlantic

Mile
108

Messum R.

Bocock's Bay

Ocean

Horing Bay C34

Cape Cross
Seal Reserve
Cape Cross

Cape C

▼28▼

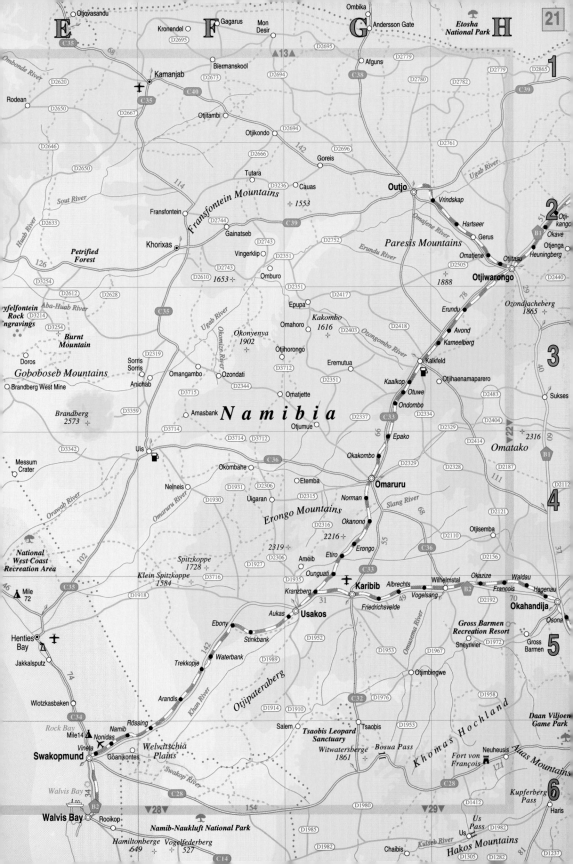

Gumare   Kandalengoti

Okavango Delta

1

Aasvoëlines

D3312

D3311

D3301

Luhebu

88

C44

Tsumkwe

Gcangwa

Mashito

Nokaneng

D3300

Qubi

D3301

Aha Hills

D3303

1250   Nxai Nxai

68

Tsau

2

Debra

Kaore

Tweeputte

D3310

Gcwihaba Hills

Gcwihaba Caverns

Molatswane

NAMIBIA

BOTSWANA

Masasara River

Bodibeng

Eiseb River

Masalanyane Pan

B o t s w a n a

3

D3301

Epukiro River

Kgabanyane Pan

Mabeleapodi Hills

Kuke

24

Tsau Hills

4

D3301

Okatuwa

D'kar

Ghanzi

D3810

Talismanis

etfontein River

D1692

Helena

Rietfontein

210

D1851

Karakubis

5

Xanagas

Tshootsha

Mamuno

Buitepos

Charles Hill

G h a n z i

Makunda

Okwa River

Tswaane

NAMIBIA

BOTSWANA

275

Gottberg

K a l a h a r i   D e s e r t

Takatswaane

6

nte

Bore

D1716

30

31

Kule

Lokalane

D3820

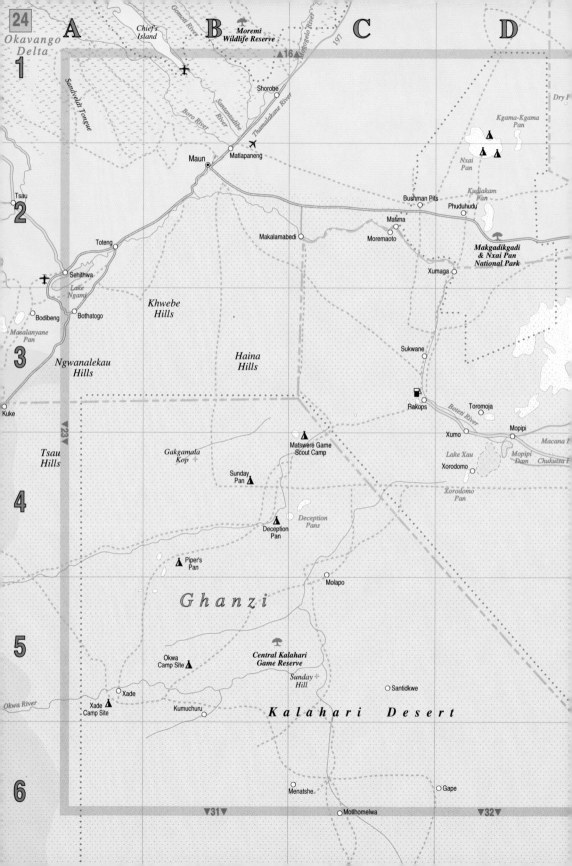

24

Okavango
Delta

A B C D

1

Chief's
Island

Gomoti River

Moremi
Wildlife Reserve

Mogogelo River

197

▲16

Dry P

Kgama-Kgama
Pan

Sandveldt Tongue

Shorobe

Boro River

Samantadibe River

Thamalakane River

Nxai
Pan

Kudiakam
Pan

2

Tsau

Maun

Matlapaneng

Bushman Pits

Phuduhudu

Matima

Makalamabedi

Moremaoto

Xumaga

Makgadikgadi
& Nxai Pan
National Park

Toteng

Sehithwa

Lake
Ngami

Khwebe
Hills

Sukwane

Bodibeng

Bothatogo

Masalanyane
Pan

Haina
Hills

3

Ngwanalekau
Hills

Rakops

Boteti River

Toromoja

Mopipi

Xumo

Macana P

Kuke

▼23▼

Tsau
Hills

Gakgamala
Kop

Matswere Game
Scout Camp

Lake Xau

Mopipi
Dam

Chukutsa P

Xorodomo

4

Sunday
Pan

Deception
Pans

Xorodomo
Pan

Deception
Pan

Piper's
Pan

Molapo

G h a n z i

5

Okwa
Camp Site

Central Kalahari
Game Reserve

Sunday
Hill

Santidkwe

Okwa River

Xade

Xade
Camp Site

Kumuchuru

K a l a h a r i   D e s e r t

6

Menatshe

Gape

▼31▼

Motlhomelwa

▼32▼

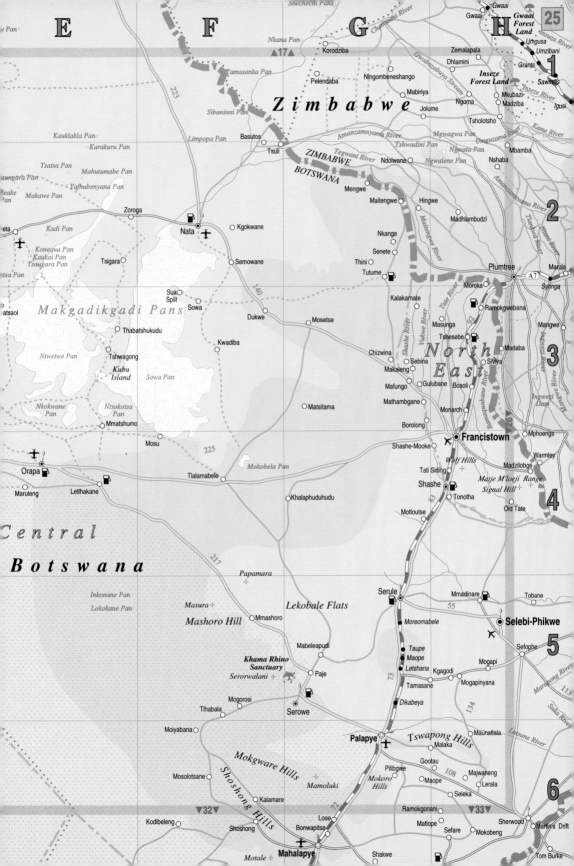

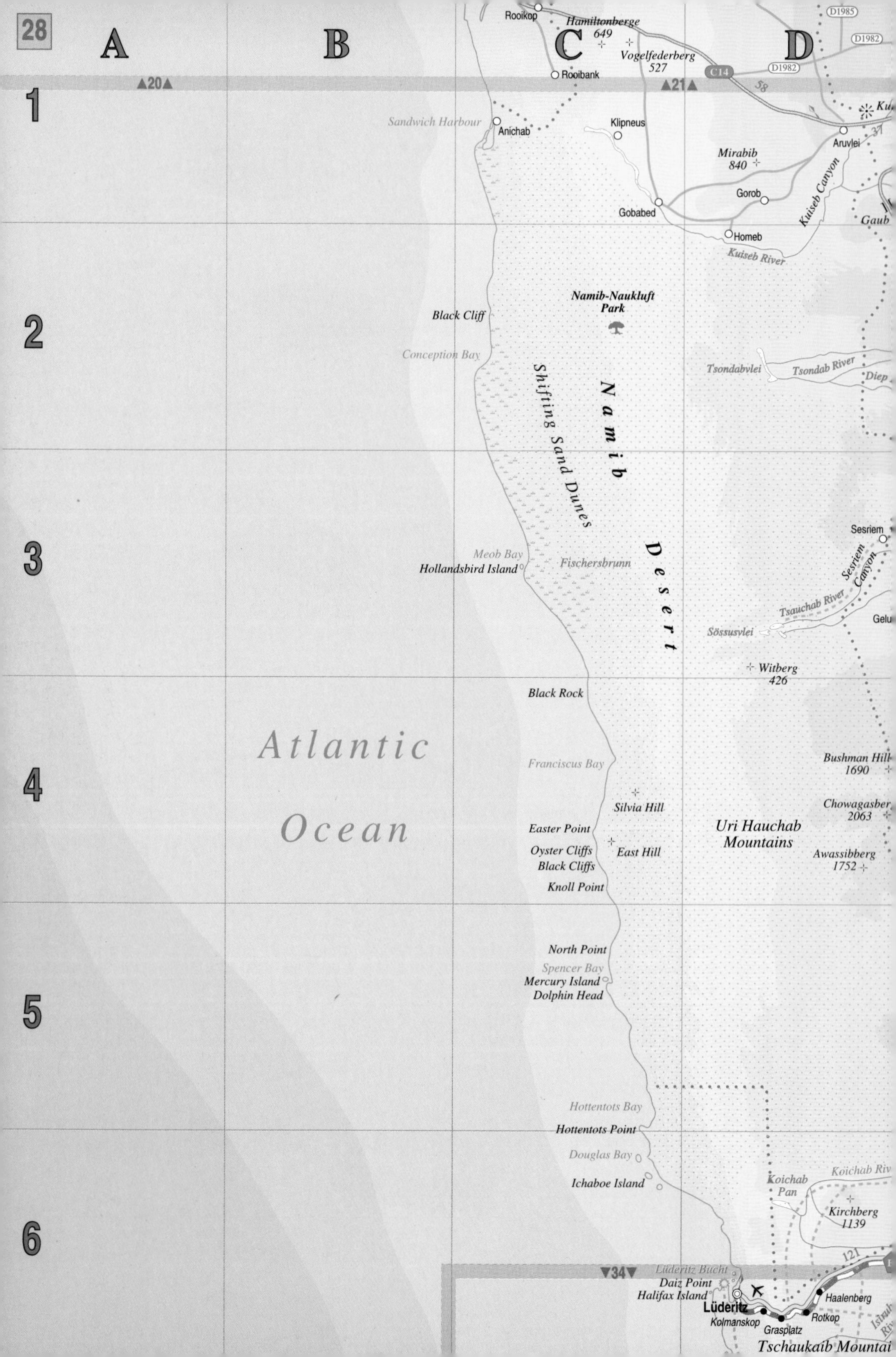

A   B   C   D

1

2

3

4

5

6

Rooikop
Hamiltonberge
649
Vogelfederberg
527
Rooibank
D1985
D1982
C14
58
D1982

Sandwich Harbour
Anichab
Klipneus
Ku
Mirabib
840
Aruvlei
Kuiseb Canyon

Gorob
Gobabed
Homeb
Gaub
Kuiseb River

Namib-Naukluft
Park

Black Cliff
Conception Bay

Tsondabvlei
Tsondab River
Diep

Shifting Sand Dunes

N
a
m
i
b

D
e
s
e
r
t

Sesriem
Meob Bay
Hollandsbird Island
Fischersbrunn

Sesriem
Canyon
Tsauchab River
Gelu
Sössusvlei

Witberg
426

Black Rock

Atlantic

Franciscus Bay
Bushman Hill
1690

Silvia Hill
Chowagasber
2063

Ocean
Easter Point
Oyster Cliffs
Black Cliffs
East Hill
Uri Hauchab
Mountains
Awassibberg
1752

Knoll Point

North Point
Spencer Bay
Mercury Island
Dolphin Head

Hottentots Bay
Hottentots Point

Douglas Bay
Ichaboe Island
Koichab Riv
Koichab
Pan
Kirchberg
1139

Lüderitz Bucht
Daiz Point
Halifax Island
Lüderitz
Kolmanskop
Grasplatz
Rotkop
Haalenberg
Tschaukaib Mountai

▲20▲   ▲21▲   ▼34▼

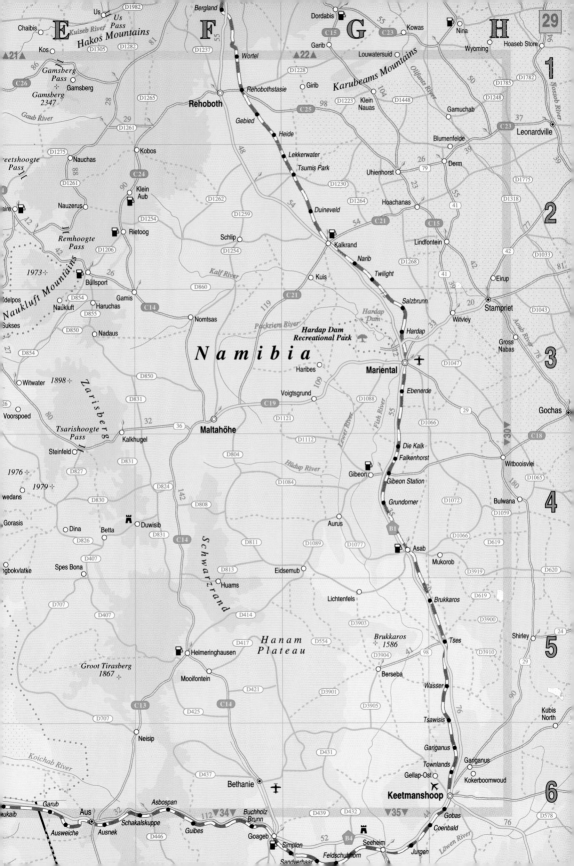

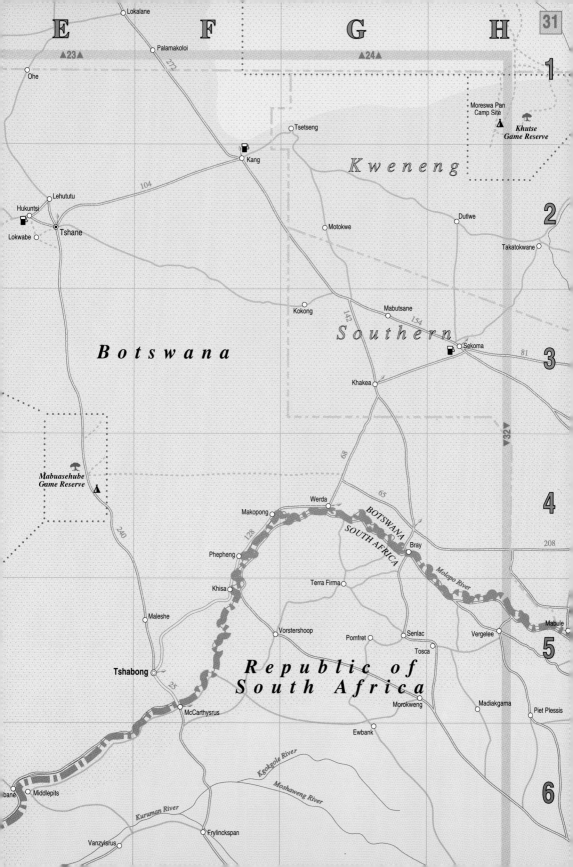

Lokalane

Palamakoloi

▲23▲   ▲24▲

Ohe

Moreswa Pan
Camp Site

*Khutse
Game Reserve*

272

K w e n e n g

Tsetseng

Kang

104

Lehututu

Dutlwe

Hukuntsi

Motokwe

Tshane

Takatokwane

Lokwabe

B o t s w a n a

S o u t h e r n

142   154

Kokong

Mabutsane

81

Sekoma

Khakea

68

▼32▼

Mabuasehube
Game Reserve

65

▲

240

BOTSWANA

Werda

SOUTH AFRICA

Makopong

Bray

128

Phepheng

208

Molapo River

Khisa

Terra Firma

Mabule

Maleshe

Vorstershoop

Senlac

Vergelee

Pomfret

R e p u b l i c o f

Tosca

Tshabong

25

S o u t h A f r i c a

McCarthysrus

Morokweng

Madiakgama

Piet Plessis

Ewbank

bane   Middlepits

Kgokgole River

Kuruman River

Moshaveng River

Vanzylsrus

Frylinckspan

A · B · C · D

1

▲24▲   ▲25▲

Kuke Pan

Botswana

Central

Bonwapitse

Motale ✝ **Mahalapye**

Sojwe
Lephephe
Dinokwe

☘ *Khutse Game Reserve*

Boatlaname

Mmamabula

Dibete ⛽

Maphashalala
Mookane
Buffelsdr

Kweneng

Kgatleng

2

Salajwe

Masama

Khudumelapye

Botlahapatlou

Artesia ⛽

Rooibok
Oliphants Drift

Takatokwane

Dikolaklolana River

Sekhukhwane River

Mmamanstwe Hill

Marico River

Mboane
Masope
Ditshegwane
Letlhakeng ⛽

62

Mahetlwe
Lentsweletau

Rasesa
Malotwana

Silent Valley

Mmankgodi

Bokaa
Mochudi

Naledi River

Gasese

Molepolole ✝

48
Metsemotlhaba River

Pilane
Odi
34

Malolwane

Oooster

81

3

Jwaneng ✝

✈

Mogoditshane

GABORONE

Tlokweng

Sikwane
Derdepoort

Dwaalboc

Thamaga

Kayaseput

Mankgodi
Mosopa
Manyana

Tlokweng Gate

Mokolodi Nature Reserve

Dwarsberg

Adriaanshoo

▲31▲

82

Mogonye ● **Ramotswa**

Zwingli

Maokane
Moshaneng
Ranaka

South East

Nietverdiend

Silkaatskop

Mabeskraa

Kanye
Ntlhantlhe

78

Matrooste

Kanye Ruins
Lotlhakane

45

Skuinsdrift

Madikwe

4

Southern

Gamoswaana

Otse

Riekertsdam
Lindleyspoort

208

Malopowabojang

Lobatse

Staatsdrif

Mmathethe ⛽

Mogojwagojwe
Digawana

Pioneer Gate

50

Gathwane
Goodhope ⛽

Metlobo

Pitsane

Dinokana

Zeerust ●

Woodbine
Groot-Marico

Swartruggens

Millval

Mokgomane

Ramathlabama ⛽

Bewley

Ottoshoop

Wondermere

Koster

5

BOTSWANA

Lead Mine

Mabule
Pitshane

SOUTH AFRICA

✈ **Mmabatho**

Tshidilamolomo

Mafikeng ●

Slurry

Rooigrond

Elandsputte
Bakerville

Carlsonia
Grootpan

Piet Plessis
Mosita

Mooifontein

Lichtenburg ●

Ventersdo

Stella

6

Sannieshof

Coligny ●

Klerksdorp ●

Ⓝ

Vryburg ●

Delareyville

Ottosdal

Orkney ●

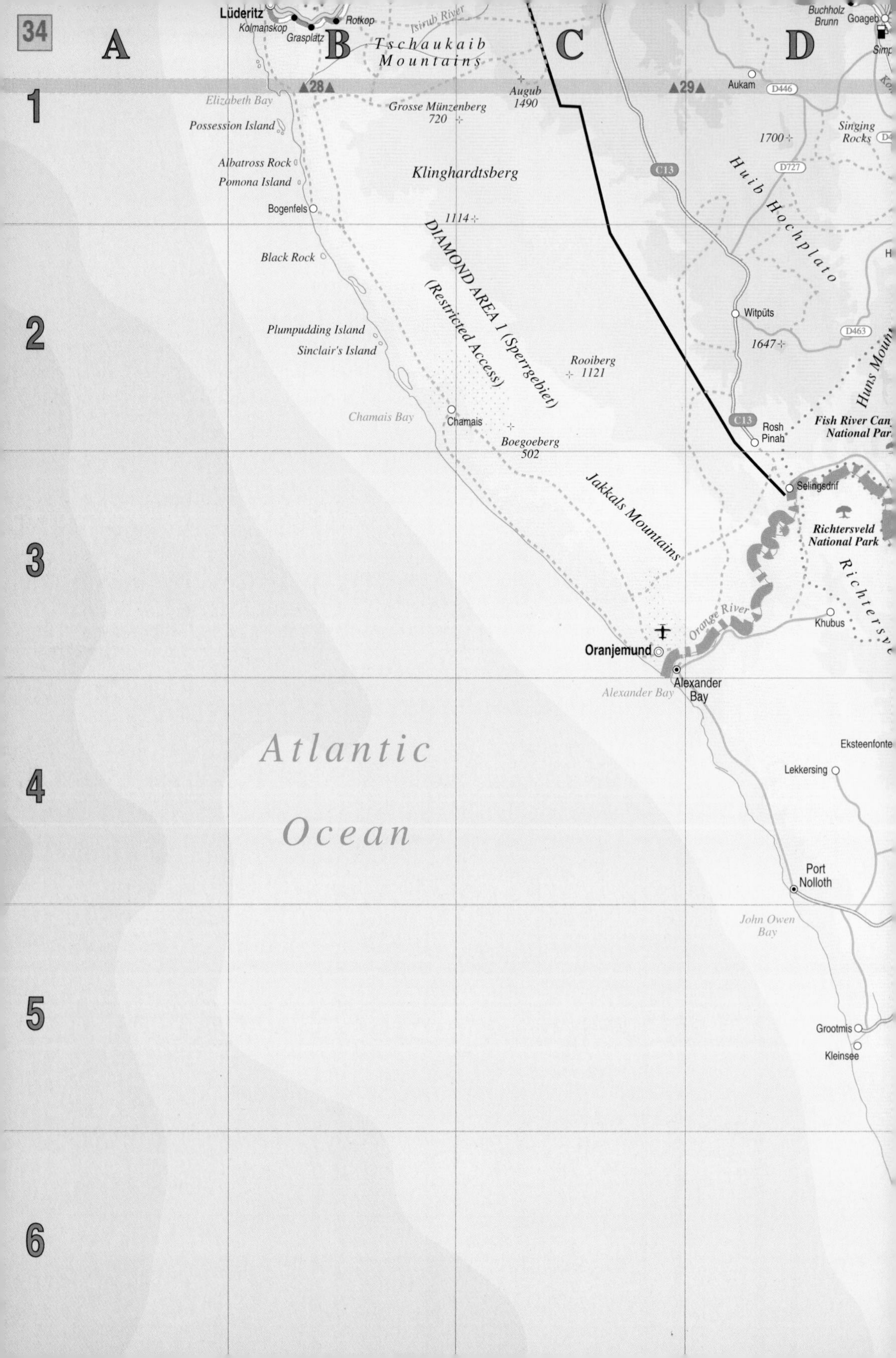

A B C D

1

2

3

4

5

6

Lüderitz
Kolmanskop • Rotkop
Grasplatz • • Grosse Münzenberg
Isirub River
Buchholz
Brunn • Goageb
Simp

*Tschaukaib
Mountains*

▲28▲

Elizabeth Bay

Possession Island

Albatross Rock •
Pomona Island

Bogenfels •

Grosse Münzenberg
720 ✛

Augub
1490

▲29▲

Aukam •
D446

Klinghardtsberg

C13

1700 ✛

*Singing
Rocks*
D4

D727

Huib Hochplato

1114 ✛

Black Rock •

DIAMOND AREA 1 (Sperrgebiet)

Witpûts •

1647 ✛

D463

Plumpudding Island •

Sinclair's Island •

(Restricted Access)

Rooiberg
1121 ✛

C13

Huns Moun

Chamais Bay

Chamais •

Boegoeberg
502

Rosh
Pinah •

*Fish River Can
National Par*

Jakkals Mountains

Selingsdrif •

*Richtersveld
National Park*

Richtersve

Orange River

Khubus •

Oranjemund ◎ ✈

Alexander Bay

● Alexander
Bay

Atlantic

Ocean

Eksteenfonte

Lekkersing •

Port
Nolloth ◎

*John Owen
Bay*

Grootmis ◎

Kleinsee •

E   **F**   **G**   **H**

52

Feldschuhhorn
Coenbald
Rietfontein

andverhaar
Jurgen
Löwen River
D578
Ganais
Aroab
Hanskeenpan

Seeheim
Naute Dam
D610
D611
D612
47
▲30▲
D622
Koppieskraalpan

1

Naute
Nordeck
Narubis
26
Warmfontein
Klipdam
Skuinskalk Pan

Gawachab
107

Charnietes
1559
Shrofenstein
2202
Vredeshoop
Obobogorap

Augrabies-Steenbok
Nature Reserve
C12
D608
D607
84
Groot Karasberge
D259
D612
Noenieput

Holoog
128
B1
D201
Tsaraxaibis
D204
Davignab

Gorges
D601
Klein Karas
154
C11
Noenieput

Hobas
Signalberg
D203
D209
D269
D205

2

Ai-Ais
D298
Grabwasser
Grünau
Nanzes
D258
Galab River

D324
Gemsvlakte
52
Kanus

C10
74
Satco
Wolpass
Nuwefontein
B3
Hamab
Kums
Ariamsvlei
Nakop

N a m i b i a
63
Karasburg
Kokerboom
N14

3

Camchab River
47
Haib
87
Hom River
103
Ham River
Langklip

D316
22
Augrabies Falls
National Park

D213
D210
Warmbad
Augrabies Falls

51
Hab River

D206
Onseepkans

Kotzehoop
Noordoewer
Bladgrond
Nabies

Vioolsdrif
NAMIBIA
SOUTH AFRICA
Goodhouse
Dabenoris
Pella

4

73
N7
Brak River
Pofadder

Steinkopf
Aggeneys
Namies
Bossiekom

Bloemhoek

Naip Noord
R e p u b l i c o f
S o u t h   A f r i c a

5

Nababeeb
Okiep
Koranderkolk

Springbok

ndeklipaai
Kamieskroom

6

Gamoep

Garies
Kliprand

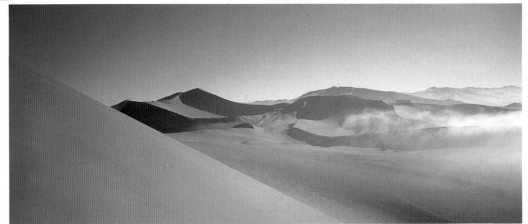

DAVID WALL

DEANNA SWANEY

DAVID WALL

Top: Namib Desert, Namibia
Middle: Himba children, Kaokoveld, North-West Namibia
Bottom: Kokerboom (Quivertree) forest near Keetmanshoop, Namibia

Getting Around Zimbabwe, Botswana & Namibia

Bus

Zimbabwe Two types of buses operate in Zimbabwe – express and local buses (also known as African buses). Express buses are relatively efficient, operating according to published timetables. Local buses go just about everywhere. The level of service and reliability varies, but they're often as quick as express buses!

Local buses can be crowded but are ultra cheap and you're more likely to meet Zimbabweans than on the express buses, which cater mainly to foreign travellers. Between major centres buses depart when full throughout the day, but for more remote destinations you need to turn up at 6 am at the latest.

Most local services depart from the *musika* or *renkini*, township markets which are outside the town centre. Larger cities and towns also have an 'in-town bus terminus'.

Botswana Botswana's surface public transport network can be summed up in two words: very limited. Bus and minibus services operate mainly through the eastern part of the country. Schedules are erratic and buses normally depart when full – naturally, it's best to turn up early in the morning. Travel by bus can be quite time-consuming and, especially along the Lobatse to Francistown route, many travellers opt to hitch or take the slow but scheduled train.

Namibia Namibian bus services aren't extensive. Luxury services are limited to journeys between Windhoek, Cape Town and Johannesburg, and there are also some involving Swakopmund, Walvis Bay and Tsumeb.

There are also local minibuses which run up and down

the B1 (the main north-south road) from Windhoek north to Oshakati and south to Keetmanshoop.

Train

Zimbabwe Zimbabwe has a good rail network connecting the major centres – Harare, Bulawayo, Victoria Falls and Mutare. They're very cheap, especially in third or economy class, which is available on all but express runs.

Most Zimbabwean trains run at night and, because of the relatively short distances, move slowly in order to arrive at a convenient hour of the morning. Sleeping compartments and bedding are inexpensive and good for a comfortable night, especially if you've been camping.

Sexes are separated at night unless you reserve a family compartment or a coupé, (two-person compartment) for an additional charge. On international trains, you must pay for food and drink in the currency of the country you are travelling through. Unless you have a coupé, (which can be locked by the conductor), leave someone to watch your gear or take it along whenever you leave the compartment.

For both domestic and international trains, you're advised to book as far ahead as possible.

Botswana Although it's slow, rail travel is a relaxing way to pass through the vast stretches of dusty and virtually featureless Botswana scrub. The railway line runs through the country between Ramokgwebana on the Zimbabwe border and Ramatlhabama on the South African border, but currently, service only extends as far south as Lobatse. The main stops are Gaborone, Mahalapye, Palapye, Serule and Francistown. There are also single-class commuter services between Gaborone, Pilane and Lobatse.

Namibia There is a reasonable rail network between most major towns but trains are slow – as one reader remarked, moving 'at the pace of an energetic donkey cart'. In addition, passenger and freight cars are mixed on the same train which tends to stop at every post.

DEANNA SWANEY

Yellow-billed Hornbill, Etosha National Park, Namibia

On the other hand, because rail travel isn't a popular mode of transport, services are rarely booked out. All trains carry economy and sleeper classes; sleepers offer four or six-bed compartments, while the very economical 3rd-class carriages have only seats. If you want a sleeper, be sure to book in advance; if there are no bookings, they don't bother to include the 1st-class carriage.

Road

Zimbabwe In a private vehicle, you can stop where you like, visit national parks at leisure and reach places not served by public transport. Motorbikes also perform well on Zimbabwe's open highways but aren't permitted in national parks.

Foreign-registered vehicles can be imported temporarily free of charge, and third-party insurance – albeit expensive – is available at the border if you're not already covered. It is also possible to bring in hire cars from Botswana, Namibia or South Africa.

A driving licence from your home country is sufficient to drive in Zimbabwe (for visits of up to 90 days), provided it's in English. Otherwise, you'll need an authenticated translation plus a photograph.

Hiring a vehicle in Zimbabwe can be expensive, so if you're on a tight budget, you'll need to be part of a group to make it worthwhile. Also, rental vehicles are in short supply, so book well in advance.

Botswana To get the most out of Botswana, you'll need a vehicle or plenty of time and patience for hitching. Road journeys in Botswana fall into one of three categories: a high-speed rush along the excellent tarred road system; an uncertain rumble over poor secondary roads; or an expedition through the wildest terrains in a sturdy, high-clearance 4WD passenger vehicle or truck.

Conventional motorbikes perform well on the tarred roads and high-powered dirt bikes can be great fun on desert tracks, but in-between are roads where clouds of dust and sand kicked up by high-speed vehicles will make for a miserable experience on a motorbike. Note that motorbikes aren't permitted in national parks or reserves.

Botswana's back roads are a maze of criss-crossing ruts and bush tracks which can utterly confound drivers. Furthermore, few of these bush roads appear on maps, many being spontaneously created routes maintained only by use. Once they become too rutted, flooded or muddy to pass, a new route is created. Indicative of changing surface conditions, multiple parallel tracks split and join, cross, wander off and back and even disappear altogether on occasion.

Hiring a vehicle – particularly a 4WD – requires a large cash outlay, but will allow you the freedom to wander and explore the best the country has to offer. Best of all, it will allow you to visit the Kalahari, which is one of Africa's most pristine wilderness areas.

Namibia By far the easiest way to get around Namibia is by road. An excellent system of tarred roads runs the entire length of the country from the South African border at Nakop and Noordoewer to Divundu in the north-east and Ruacana in the north-west.

Similarly, tarred spur roads connect the main north-south arteries to Gobabis, Lüderitz, Swakopmund and Walvis Bay. Around the rest of the country, most towns and sites are connected by good gravel roads. As a general rule, B and C-numbered highways are well maintained and passable to all vehicles. D-numbered roads may be a bit rougher but are often passable to 2WD vehicles. However, driving on gravel roads can be at best tricky and at worst treacherous – be careful. Note that motorbikes aren't permitted in any of the national

DAVID WALL

Left: Zebra, Etosha National Park, Namibia
Right: Victoria Falls, Zimbabwe

DAVID WALL

parks, with the exception of the main routes through Namib-Naukluft park.

Car hire is expensive, but if you have a group, it's the best and most straightforward way of seeing the country. Book your car well in advance.

Bicycle

Zimbabwe Major routes in Zimbabwe are surfaced and in excellent repair, and road shoulders are often sealed and separated from the mainstream of vehicular traffic by painted yellow lines, so they could be used as bicycle lanes. It's important to note, however, that bicycles are not permitted in game parks.

Very little is available in terms of spares, not even in Harare, so bring all the tools and spares you anticipate needing.

Botswana Botswana is largely flat but that's the only concession it makes to cyclists. Unless you know what you're doing, abandon any ideas you may have about a Botswana bicycle adventure. Distances are great, horizons are vast; the climate and landscape are hot and dry; the sun is intense through the clear and semi-tropical desert air; and even along major routes, water is scarce and villages are widely spaced.

On the flat and straight tarred roads, the national speed limit of 110 km/h doesn't prevent traffic cranking up the speed and when a semitrailer passes at 150 km/h, cyclists may unwittingly be blown off the road. To access areas off the beaten track, bicycles are also unsuitable – even experienced cyclists have pronounced most of the country's roads and tracks uncyclable. Along untarred roads, vehicles howl past in billowing clouds of sand and dust, and on lesser-used routes, you're likely to encounter deep drifted sand. Unless you're prepared to carry your bike and luggage over long, uninhabited distances, don't venture off main routes. Also bear in mind that bicycles are not permitted in Botswana's wildlife reserves.

Namibia Terrain-wise, Namibia's wide-open spaces are generally amenable for cyclists, but remember that distances between villages are vast and water is generally scarce, so carry ample supplies. Also, climatic conditions can be harsh, ranging from sweltering hot and dry to windy with heavy fog or blowing sand.

Again, bicycles are not permitted inside national parks or game reserves.

Boat

Zimbabwe Since Zimbabwe is a landlocked country, the only boats of any consequence are two ferry systems that operate on Lake Kariba between Kariba town and Binga or Mlibizi near the western end of the lake. They're handy especially if you want to do a circular tour of Zimbabwe without retracing your steps between Victoria Falls and Bulawayo.

DEANNA SWANEY

Himba mother and child, Kaokoveld, North-West Namibia

Comment Circuler au Zimbabwe, au Botswana et en Namibie

FRANÇAIS

Bus

Zimbabwe Il existe deux catégories de bus, les express et les locaux (ou bus africains). Le réseau express fonctionne relativement bien, en respectant des horaires établis. Les bus locaux vont quasiment partout. Si leur confort et leur fiabilité restent variables, ils sont souvent plus rapides que les express.

Parfois bondés, ils sont néanmoins très bon marché et il y est plus facile de rencontrer des gens du pays que dans les express. Les bus à destination des grandes villes partent tout au long de la journée, dès qu'ils sont pleins. Mais si vous vous

rendez dans une localité plus reculée, présentez-vous à l'arrêt à 6h du matin au plus tard.

La plupart des lignes locales partent du *musika* ou du *renkini*, marchés des townships se trouvant à l'extérieur de la ville. Dans les villes relativement importantes, on trouve également des gares routières centrales (in-town bus terminus).

Botswana Le réseau des transports publics du Botswana se résume en deux mots : très limité. Seul l'est du pays, ou presque, est desservi par un service de bus et de minibus. Les horaires sont plutôt fantasques,

DEANNA SWANEY

Young Herero boy, Kaokoveld, North-West Namibia

les bus partent généralement lorsqu'ils sont pleins. Il est donc conseillé d'arriver tôt le matin. Comme les trajets en bus peuvent être très longs, notamment entre Lobatse et Francistown, beaucoup de voyageurs préfèrent tenter le stop ou prendre le train ; ce dernier est lent mais régulier.

Namibie Le réseau de bus namibien est loin d'être très développé. Les services de luxe assurent uniquement les liaisons entre Windhoek, Le Cap et Johannesburg, certains desservant également Swakopmund, Walvis Bay et Tsumeb.

Quelques minibus locaux au départ de Windhoek font par ailleurs la navette par la B 1 (principal axe nord-sud) sur Oshakati au nord et Keetmanshoop au sud.

Train

Zimbabwe Le réseau ferroviaire du Zimbabwe dessert les principaux centres touristiques : Harare, Bulawayo, les chutes Victoria et Mutare. Les voyages en train sont bon marché, notamment en troisième classe. Cette classe économique est disponible sur tous les trains sauf les express.

La plupart des trains circulent de nuit et, en raison des distances relativement courtes, progressent lentement afin d'arriver à une heure décente le matin. Les compartiments couchettes sont peu coteux et confortables, surtout après quelques nuits de camping.

La nuit, les hommes et les femmes sont séparés, sauf si l'on réserve un compartiment familial ou un coupé (compartiment à deux places) moyennant un supplément. Sur le réseau international, vous devrez payer votre nourriture et vos boissons dans la monnaie du pays que vous traversez. Si vous n'occupez pas un coupé (qui peut être verrouillé par le contrôleur), demandez à quelqu'un de surveiller vos affaires ou emmenez ces dernières avec vous lorsque vous quittez le compartiment.

Que vous empruntiez une ligne nationale ou internationale, réservez le plus longtemps possible à l'avance.

Botswana Malgré leur lenteur, les trains permettent de traverser agréablement les immenses étendues de poussière sans grand intérêt qui couvrent une grande partie du Botswana. L'unique voie ferrée du pays relie Ramokgwebana, à la frontière avec le Zimbabwe, à Ramatlhabama, à la frontière sud-africaine. Au sud, le service s'arrête en fait à Lobatse. Les principales gares desservies sont Gaborone, Mahalapye, Palapye, Serule et Francistown. Plusieurs navettes de classe unique relient également Gaborone, Pilane et Lobatse.

Namibie Le réseau ferroviaire namibien dessert la plupart des villes principales, mais les trains sont lents. Comme le faisait remarquer un lecteur, 'ils circulent à la vitesse d'une charrette tirée par un âne dynamique'. De plus, les voitures de voyageurs et de marchandises étant convoyées en même temps, ils ont tendance à s'arrêter dans toutes les gares.

En revanche, il est rare de ne pas trouver de place car ce n'est pas un moyen de transport très couru. La classe économique et les couchettes sont disponibles sur tous les trains. En couchette, vous avez le choix entre des compartiments à quatre ou six lits, mais les voitures de la très économique troisième classe n'offrent que des fauteuils. Si vous désirez une couchette, réservez à l'avance car s'il n'y a aucune réservation, les cheminots ne prennent pas la peine d'installer la première classe.

Route

Zimbabwe Circuler en voiture particulière permet de s'arrêter où l'on veut, de visiter les parcs nationaux à loisir et d'accéder aux sites non desservis par les transports publics. La moto est également agréable sur les grandes routes mais elle est interdite dans les réserves.

L'importation des véhicules immatriculés à l'étranger est autorisée à titre temporaire et gratuit, une assurance au tiers (très chère) pouvant être délivrée à la frontière à ceux qui ne sont pas déjà couverts. Il est également possible d'arriver avec une voiture de location depuis le Botswana, la Namibie ou l'Afrique du Sud.

Le permis de conduire de votre pays d'origine suffit (pour les séjours de 90 jours au plus), à condition qu'il soit en anglais. Dans le cas contraire, vous devrez vous munir d'une traduction authentifiée et d'une photo ou encore d'un permis de conduire international (délivré dans votre préfecture).

La location d'un véhicule peut revenir très cher au Zimbabwe. Si vous disposez d'un budget serré, mieux vaut vous intégrer à un groupe, sinon cela ne vaut pas le coup. Le parc automobile étant par ailleurs assez limité, il est conseillé de faire les réservations longtemps à l'avance.

Botswana Pour profiter au mieux du pays, vous aurez besoin soit d'un véhicule, soit de beaucoup de temps et de patience pour faire du stop. Si vous voyagez par la route, vous aurez le choix entre des déplacements rapides sur un excellent réseau routier goudronné, une progression plus aventureuse sur des routes secondaires cahoteuses ou une véritable expédition en brousse dans un solide 4x4 ou en camion.

Sur les routes goudronnées, on roule très bien avec une moto routière et sur les pistes du désert on peut vraiment se faire plaisir avec les grosses cylindrées enduro. Mais il existe aussi de nombreuses routes sur lesquelles la moto devient un véritable cauchemar à cause des nuages de poussière et de sable projetés par les autres véhicules. Notez que les motos ne pas admises dans les réserves ni dans les parcs nationaux.

Le réseau secondaire forme un véritable labyrinthe de chemins défoncés et de pistes de brousse où l'on se perd facilement. Ces pistes sont en outre rarement indiquées sur les cartes, la plupart étant créées spontanément et seulement maintenues par le passage des véhicules. Dès qu'elles deviennent impraticables à cause des ornières, des inondations ou de la boue, les voies parallèles se multiplient, se séparant, se rejoignant ou se croisant avant de s'effacer par endroit ou de disparaître totalement.

Pour louer un véhicule, notamment un 4x4, il vous faudra disposer d'une importante somme en espèce, mais cet investissement vous permettra ensuite d'explorer en toute liberté les plus beaux coins du pays. Par-dessus tout, vous pourrez visiter le désert du Kalahari, l'une des régions sauvages les mieux préservées de toute l'Afrique.

Namibie La route offre de loin le moyen de transport le plus pratique. Un excellent réseau de voies goudronnées couvre l'étendue du pays de Nakop, à la frontière sud-africaine, à Noordoewer et Divundu au nord-est et Ruacana au nord-ouest.

Parallèlement, de petites routes goudronnées relient les principales artères nord-sud à Gobabis, Lüderitz, Swakopmund et Walvis Bay. Dans le reste du pays, la plupart des villes et des sites sont desservis par des routes gravillonnées en bon état. En règle générale, les

DEANNA SWANEY

DEANNA SWANEY

Left: Elephants, Hwange National Park, Zimbabwe
Right: Drowned tree, Matusadona National Park, Zimbabwe

voies numérotées B et C sont bien entretenues et praticables par tous les types de véhicule. Si les voies D sont souvent plus mauvaises, on peut néanmoins y circuler avec un véhicule standard à deux roues motrices. Les routes de gravier peuvent en revanche s'avérer difficiles, voire traîtres, soyez prudent. Sachez que les motos sont interdites dans tous les parcs nationaux, à l'exception des routes principales traversant le parc de Namib-Naukluft.

La location d'une voiture revient très cher, mais si vous êtes en groupe, c'est le moyen le plus simple et le plus rapide de visiter le pays. Faites vos réservations longtemps à l'avance.

Bicyclette

Zimbabwe Les routes principales goudronnées sont en excellent état et les accotements souvent séparés de la chaussée par des lignes peintes en jaune, de sorte qu'ils peuvent servir de pistes cyclables. Il est néanmoins interdit de circuler à bicyclette dans les réserves naturelles.

Les pièces détachées étant rares, même à Harare, n'oubliez pas de vous munir des outils et des pièces dont vous pensez avoir éventuellement besoin.

Botswana Le pays est en grande partie plat, mais c'est bien là la seule concession qu'il fait aux cyclistes. A moins d'être inconscient, laissez tomber l'idée de vous lancer dans une expédition à deux roues au Botswana. Les distances sont longues, l'horizon s'étend à perte de vue, le climat est plutôt chaud et sec, le soleil tape très fort sur le désert semi-tropical et, même le long des routes principales, l'eau est rare et les villages très espacés.

Sur les routes goudronnées droites et plates, la vitesse est limitée à 110 km/h, ce qui n'empêche pas certains semi-remorques de dépasser les cyclistes à 150 km/h ; il faut donc bien se cramponner à son guidon. La bicyclette ne se prête guère non plus aux excursions hors des sentiers battus. Selon les randonneurs les plus expérimentés, la plupart des routes et des pistes du Botswana sont impraticables. Sur les routes non goudronnées, les véhicules passent à toute vitesse en déplaçant d'énormes nuages de poussière et de sable et, sur les routes moins fréquentées, vous avez toutes les chances de vous casser le nez sur de profondes plaques de sable. A moins d'être prêt à porter votre "petite reine"

et vos bagages sur de longues distances sans rencontrer âme qui vive, ne vous aventurez pas hors des routes principales. N'oubliez pas non plus que la bicyclette est interdite dans les réserves naturelles du Botswana.

Namibie Sur le plan purement géographique, les vastes espaces namibiens se prêtent tout à fait à la pratique du vélo, mais les distances entre les villages sont très longues et l'eau est souvent rare, il faut donc prévoir des réserves. Par ailleurs, les conditions climatiques peuvent être dures car on peut passer d'un temps très chaud et sec à un épais brouillard balayé par des vents assez forts ou des tempêtes de sable.

Là encore, les bicyclettes ne sont pas autorisées dans les parcs nationaux ni dans les réserves naturelles.

Bateau

Zimbabwe Le pays ne disposant d'aucun accès à la mer, les seuls bateaux importants sont les bacs qui assurent la liaison, sur le lac Kariba, entre Kariba town et Binga ou Mlibizi, près de la rive ouest. Ils sont surtout pratiques pour faire le tour du pays sans revenir sur ses pas entre les chutes Victoria et Bulawayo.

Reisen in Simbabwe, Botswana und Namibia

DEUTSCH
Per Bus

Simbabwe Es gibt in Simbabwe zwei Arten von Bussen – Expreß-und Nahverkehrsbusse (auch bekannt als afrikanische Busse). Expreßbusse sind relativ effizient und richten sich nach veröffentlichten Fahrplänen. Nahverkehrsbusse fahren fast überall hin. Service und Zuverlässigkeit mögen unterschiedlich sein, doch sie sind oft genauso schnell wie Expreßbusse!

Nahverkehrsbusse können überfüllt sein, sind jedoch extrem preiswert. Man trifft in ihnen viel eher Einheimische als in den Expreßbussen, die hauptsächlich auf ausländische Touristen zugeschnitten sind. Zwischen den Hauptzentren fahren Busse tagsüber ab wenn voll; für Busse nach abgelegeneren Zielorten findet man sich spätestens um 6 Uhr morgens ein.

Die meisten Nahverkehrsdienste fahren von *musika* oder *renkini* ab, Dorfmärkten, die sich außerhalb der Dorfmitte befinden. Größere Gemeinden und Städte haben auch eine Bus-Haupthaltestelle in der Stadt selbst.

Botswana Botswanas öffentliches Landtransportnetz kann in zwei Worten beschrieben werden: Sehr beschränkt. Bus- und Minibusdienste stehen hauptsächlich durch den östlichen Teil des Landes zur Verfügung. Die Fahrdienste sind unregelmäßig, und die Busse fahren normalerweise ab wenn voll – natürlich findet man sich am besten früh am Morgen ein. Das Reisen mit dem Bus kann sehr zeitraubend sein, so daß sich besonders entlang der Lobatse-Francistown-Route viele Touristen für das Reisen per Anhalter entscheiden oder den langsamen, jedoch fahrplanmäßigen Zug nehmen.

Namibia Der Busdienst in Namibia ist nicht weitreichend. Luxusdienste sind auf Reisen zwischen Windhoek, Kapstadt und Johannesburg beschränkt. Manche betreuen außerdem noch Swakopmund, Walvis Bay und Tsumeb.

Dazu gibt es Nahverkehrs-Minibusse, die die B1 (die Haupt-Nordsüdstraße) von Windhoek nach Oshakati im Norden und nach Keetmanshoop im Süden befahren.

Per Zug

Simbabwe Simbabwe verfügt über ein gutes, die Hauptzentren Harare, Bulawayo, Victoria Falls und Mutare verbindendes Schienennetz. Züge sind sehr preisgünstig, besonders in dritter oder Economy-Klasse, die bei allen Zügen außer Expreßverbindungen erhältlich sind.

Die meisten Züge fahren nachts und sind aufgrund der relativ kurzen Entfernungen langsam, so daß sie zu annehmbarer Zeit am Morgen ankommen.

Schlafabteile und Bettzeug sind recht erschwinglich und gestatten besonders nach Zelterfahrungen eine bequeme Nacht.

Des nachts werden die Geschlechter getrennt, es sei denn, man reserviert ein Familienabteil oder ein Coupé (Abteil für zwei Personen) zu einem Extrazuschlag. In internationalen Zügen ist die Verpflegung in der Währung des Landes zu bezahlen, das gerade durchreist wird. Außer Sie haben ein Coupé gemietet (das vom Schaffner abgeschlossen werden kann), lassen Sie am besten jemand bei Ihren Sachen zurück oder nehmen sie mit, wenn immer Sie das Abteil verlassen.

Für inländische und internationale Züge empfiehlt sich frühstmögliche Reservierung.

Botswana Obgleich langsam, ist das Reisen im Zug eine angenehme Art, die weiten Gebiete staubigen und praktisch nichtssagenden Buschlands zu durchqueren. Die Zuglinie durchzieht das Land zwischen Ramokgwebana an der Grenze zu Simbabwe und Ramatlhabama an der südafrikanischen Grenze. Momentan jedoch führt der Dienst nur bis Lobatse im Süden. Die Hauptstationen sind Gaborone, Mahalapye, Palapye, Serule und Francistown. Pendlerdienste mit nur einer Klasse operieren zwischen Gaborone, Pilane und Lobatse.

Namibia Die meisten größeren Städte werden von einem annehmbaren Schienennetz bedient, doch die Züge sind

DAVID WALL

Ostrich, Matobo National Park, Zimbabwe

langsam. Wie ein Leser bemerkte, bewegen sie sich 'im Tempo eines energischen Eselkarrens'. Zusätzlich bestehen Züge aus Passagierwagen und Frachtwaggons und halten oft allerorts.

Da der Zug kein beliebtes Reisemittel darstellt, sind die Dienste auf der anderen Seite selten ausgebucht. Alle Züge besitzen Economy-und Schlafwagenklassen; Schlafwagen bieten Abteile mit vier oder sechs Betten, während die sehr wirtschaftlichen Wagen der dritten Klasse nur über Sitze verfügen. Wollen Sie ein Schlafabteil, so reservieren Sie am besten im voraus; wenn keine Reservierungen gemacht wurden, wird der Erste-Klasse-Wagen nicht angehängt.

Straße

Simbabwe Mit einem Privatwagen können Sie anhalten, wo Sie wollen, nach Belieben Nationalparks besuchen und Orte erreichen, die nicht vom öffentlichen Verkehrssystem versorgt werden. Auch Motorräder sind gut für die offenen Hauptverkehrsstraßen des Landes geeignet, allerdings in Nationalparks nicht gestattet.

Fahrzeuge mit ausländischen Nummernschildern können zeitweise kostenlos importiert werden; an der Grenze kann man eine (wenn auch kostspielige) Haftpflichtversicherung abschließen, wenn man nicht schon entsprechend versorgt ist. Es ist auch möglich, Mietwagen aus Botswana, Namibia oder Südafrika ins Land zu bringen.

Vorausgesetzt, er ist in englischer Sprache abgefaßt, genügt ein in Ihrem Heimatland ausgestellter Führerschein für Simbabwe (für Besuchszeiten bis zu 90 Tagen). Ansonsten benötigen Sie eine beglaubigte Übersetzung und ein Foto.

In Simbabwe kann das Automieten teuer sein. Wenn Sie also wenig Geld zur Verfügung haben, lohnt sich diese Option erst in einer Gruppe. Außerdem sind Mietfahrzeuge nicht im Überfluß vorhanden, so daß es sich empfiehlt, lange im voraus zu buchen.

Botswana Um den besten Eindruck von Botswana zu bekommen, brauchen Sie ein Fahrzeug oder viel Zeit und Geduld fürs Trampen. Autoreisen in Botswana fallen in eine von drei Kategorien: Ein Dahinjagen auf dem ausgezeichneten Teerstraßensystem; ein unsicheres Rumpeln über schlechte Nebenstraßen, oder eine Expedition durch das wildeste Gelände in einem robusten Gelände-oder Lastwagen mit hoher Bodenfreiheit.

Konventionelle Motorräder sind gut für die geteerten Straßen geeignet. Mit starkmotorigen Geländerädern kann man zwar auf Wüstenstraßen viel Spaß haben, doch gibt es dazwischen Straßen, wo von Hochgeschwindigkeitsfahrzeugen aufgewirbelte Staub-und Sandwolken das Motorradfahren zu einer ausgesprochenen Tortur machen. Beachten Sie bitte, daß Motorräder in Nationalparks oder Reservaten nicht gestattet sind.

Botswanas Landstraßen bilden ein Gewirr kreuz und quer verlaufender Furchen und Buschwege, das den Fahrer vollkommen durcheinanderbringen kann. Wenige dieser Buschrouten sind außerdem auf Landkarten verzeichnet, da viele spontan geschaffen und nur durch Benutzung unterhalten werden. Werden sie einmal zu ausgefurcht, überschwemmt oder zu schlammig zum Befahren, wird eine neue Route geschaffen. Viele parallele Wege teilen sich, treffen wieder aufeinander, kreuzen sich, wandern ab und wieder zurück und verschwinden sogar gelegentlich ganz gemäß sich ändernder Oberflächenzustände.

Zum Mieten eines Fahrzeuges, besonders eines Geländewagens, ist zwar eine Menge Bargeld vorzustrecken, doch erwerben Sie damit die Freiheit, die schönsten Stellen des Landes zu erreichen und zu entdecken. Am allerbesten: Sie können damit die Kalahari besuchen, eines der unberührtesten Gebiete der afrikanischen Wildnis.

Namibia Namibia ist auf bei weitem einfachste Weise per Straße zu erkunden. Ein ausgezeichnetes Teerstraßensystem erstreckt sich über die gesamte Länge des Landes von der südafrikanischen Grenze bei Nakop und Noordoewer bis Divundu im Nordosten und Ruacana im Nordwesten.

Ähnlich verbinden geteerte Nebenstraßen die Haupt-Nordsüdarterien nach Gobabis, Lüderitz, Swakopmund und Walvis Bay. Im restlichen Land sind die meisten Städte und Orte mit guten Schotterstraßen verbunden. Hauptverkehrsstraßen mit vorgestelltem B und C sind im allgemeinen in gutem Zustand und mit allen Fahrzeugen befahrbar. Straßen mit vorgestelltem D können etwas holpriger sein, sind jedoch oft für zweiradgetriebene Fahrzeuge geeignet. Das Fahren auf Schotterstraßen kann jedoch im besten Falle heikel und im schlimmsten trügerisch sein – also Vorsicht. Beachten Sie, daß Motorräder in keinem der Nationalparks mit Ausnahme der Hauptrouten durch den Namib-Naukluft-Park zugelassen sind.

Ein Auto zu mieten ist teuer, jedoch für eine Gruppe die beste und einfachste Art, das Land zu erkunden. Reservieren Sie Ihr Auto lange im voraus.

Per Fahrrad

Simbabwe Die Decken der Hauptstraßen in Simbabwe sind in ausgezeichnetem Zustand. Die Straßenränder sind oft befestigt und durch aufgemalte gelbe Linien vom Hauptverkehrsfluß getrennt, so daß sie als Fahrradspuren benutzt werden können. Wichtig zu beachten ist, daß Fahrräder in Wildparks nicht gestattet sind.

Ersatzteile sind auch in Harare kaum erhältlich, so daß Sie am besten alle Werkzeuge und Ersatzteile mitbringen, die Sie zu benötigen erwarten.

Botswana Botswana ist großenteils flach; doch das ist das einzige Zugeständnis, das das Land Radfahrern gegenüber macht. Es sei denn, Sie wissen, was Sie tun, geben Sie besser alle Vorstellungen auf, die Sie von einem Radabenteuer in Botswana haben mögen. Die Entfernungen sind groß, die Horizonte weit; Klima und Landschaft sind heiß und trocken; die Sonne brennt stark durch die klare subtropische Wüstenluft, und auch entlang der Hauptrouten ist Wasser knapp, und die Dörfer sind weit verstreut.

Auf den flachen und geraden Teerstraßen hält die nationale Geschwindigkeitsbegrenzung von 110 km/h den Verkehr nicht davon ab, das Tempo hochzuschrauben. Wenn ein Sattelschlepper mit 150 km/h vorbeibraust, kann er Radfahrer unbeabsichtigt von der Straße fegen.

Fahrräder sind außerdem ungeeignet zum Erreichen von abgelegenen Gebieten – auch erfahrene Radfahrer haben den Großteil der Straßen und Wege des Landes für unbenutzbar erklärt. Auf ungeteerten Straßen heulen Fahrzeuge in aufgewirbelten Sand- und Staubwolken vorbei, und auf weniger benutzten Routen werden Sie wahrscheinlich auf tiefe Sandwehen stoßen. Es sei denn, Sie sind bereit, Fahrrad und Gepäck über lange menschenleere Entfernungen zu tragen, bleiben Sie besser auf den Hauptstraßen.

Fahrräder sind in Botswanas Tierreservaten nicht zugelassen.

Namibia Was das Terrain anbetrifft, so ist Namibias offene Weite im allgemeinen Radfahrern wohlgesonnen, doch vergessen Sie nicht, daß die Entfernungen zwischen Dörfern groß sind und Wasser im allgemeinen knapp ist. Versorgen Sie sich daher ausreichend damit. Das Klima kann harsch sein und von drückend heiß und trocken bis windig mit dichtem Nebel oder aufgewirbeltem Sand reichen. Auch hier sind Fahrräder weder in Nationalparks noch in Wildreservaten gestattet.

Per Schiff
Simbabwe Da Simbabwe landumschlossen ist, gehören die einzigen Schiffe von Bedeutung zu zwei Fährensystemen, die auf dem Kariba-See zwischen der Stadt Kariba und Binga oder Mlibizi am westlichen Ende des Sees operieren. Sie kommen besonders dann gelegen, wenn Sie eine Rundreise durch Simbabwe unternehmen wollen ohne zwischen Victoria Falls und Bulawayo den gleichen Weg noch einmal zurücklegen zu müssen.

DEANNA SWANEY

DEANNA SWANEY

Top: Hartebeest, Chief's Island, Moremi Wildlife Reserve, Botswana
Bottom: Warthog, Chief's Island, Moremi Wildlife Reserve, Botswana

Cómo Movilizarse dentro de Zimbabwe, Botswana y Namibia

ESPAÑOL

En Autobús

Zimbabwe En Zimbabwe operan dos tipos de autobuses: los expresos y los locales (también conocidos como autobuses africanos). Los autobuses expresos son relativamente eficientes y operan de acuerdo a los horarios publicados. Los autobuses locales van prácticamente a todas partes. El nivel y la confiabilidad del servicio varían, pero son generalmente tan rápidos como los autobuses expresos.

Los autobuses locales generalmente van muy apiñados, pero son super-baratos y uno tiene mayores posibilidades de conocer zimbabwenses que en los autobuses expresos los cuales, generalmente, son utilizados por viajeros extranjeros. Entre los centros de mayor importancia, durante el día, los autobuses salen cuando se han llenado, pero para los que van hacia lugares más remotos se necesita llegar a la estación a más tardar a las 6 de la mañana.

La mayoría de los servicios locales salen de la *musika* o *renkini*, que son los mercados de los pueblos, localizados afuera del centro de los mismos. Las ciudades y los pueblos más grandes también tienen 'terminales de autobuses'.

Botswana El servicio de transporte público de Botswana puede resumirse en dos palabras: *muy limitado*. Los servicios de autobuses y minibuses operan principalmente a través de la parte este del país. Los itinerarios son erráticos y los autobuses normalmente salen cuando se han llenado – naturalmente que es mejor llegar temprano por la mañana. El viaje en autobús puede llevar mucho tiempo y, especialmente en la ruta de Lobatse a Francistown, muchos viajeros optan por "echar dedo" o tomar el tren que es lento pero que viaja con horario.

Namibia Los servicios de autobuses de Namibia no son extensos. Los servicios de lujo se limitan a viajes entre Windhoek, Ciudad del Cabo y Johannesburgo, y también algunos otros que comprenden Swakopmund, Bahía Walbis y Tsumeb.

También hay minibuses locales que recorren de arriba a abajo la B1(que es la carretera principal que va de norte a sur) de Windhoek norte a Oshakati y al sur a Keetmanshoop.

En Tren

Zimbabwe Tiene una buena red de ferrocarril que conecta los centros principales: Harare, Bulawayo, las Cataratas Victoria y Mutare. Los pasajes son muy baratos especialmente en la tercera clase (o económica), que se puede obtener en todos los trenes excepto en los expresos.

La mayoría de los trenes de Zimbabwe viajan de noche y, debido a las distancias que son relativamente cortas, viajan lentamente para llegar a una hora conveniente por la mañana. Las cabinas dormitorio y los servicios de cama no son caros y son buenos para pasar la noche cómodamente, especialmente cuando se ha estado acampando.

Los sexos son separados por la noche, a menos que se reserve un compartimiento familiar o un coupé (cabina para dos personas) con un pago adicional.

DAVID WALL

Waterbuck, Okavango Delta, Botswana

En los trenes internacionales hay que pagar por las comidas y bebidas en la moneda del país por el que se esté viajando. A menos que se tenga una cabina coupé (que puede ser cerrada con llave por el conductor) se debe dejar a alguien cuidando las pertenencias (o llevarlas consigo) al alejarse de la cabina.

Tanto para los trenes domésticos como para los internacionales se recomienda hacer reservaciones con la mayor anticipación posible.

Botswana Aunque lento, el viaje por tren es una manera muy relajante de pasar por las vastas zonas polvorientas y virtualmente sin panorama de Botswana. La línea ferroviaria atraviesa el país entre Ramokgwebana en la frontera con Zimbabwe y Ramatlhabama en la frontera con Sur Africa pero, actualmente, el servicio hacia el sur solamente va hasta Lobatse. Las paradas principales son Gaborone, Mahalapye, Palapye, Serule y Francistown. También hay servicios de pasajeros de una sola clase entre Gaborne, Pilane y Lobatse.

Namibia Hay una red ferroviaria razonable entre la mayoría de las poblaciones importantes pero los trenes son lentos – como comentó un lector, 'se mueven al paso de un carro tirado por un burro energético'. Además los trenes son mixtos: pasajeros y carga en el mismo tren, que tiene la tendencia a detenerse en todos los sitios.

Por otra parte, debido a que el viaje por tren no es muy popular, los cupos rara vez se agotan. Todos los trenes tienen clases de economía y dormitorios; los dormitorios ofrecen cabinas de cuatro o seis camas, mientras que los más económicos de tercera clase solo tienen asientos. Si desea un dormitorio debe reservarlo con anticipación; si no hay reser-

vaciones, no se toman la molestia de incluir el coche de primera clase.

Por Carretera

Zimbabwe En un vehículo privado usted se puede detener en cualquier parte, visitar los parques nacionales tomándose el tiempo que quiera y se puede llegar a lugares a donde no llega el transporte público. Las motocicletas también rinden bien en las autopistas libres de Zimbabwe, aunque no son admitidas en los parques nacionales.

Temporalmente y gratuitamente se permite entrar a los vehículos registrados en el extranjero, y el seguro contra terceros, aunque caro, se puede obtener en la frontera, si no se tiene ya. También es posible entrar vehículos alquilados de Botswana, Namibia y Sud Africa.

La licencia de conducir del país de procedencia es suficiente para conducir en Zimbabwe (por visitas de hasta 90 días), siempre y cuando esté en inglés. De otro modo, se requiere una traducción autenticada y una fotografía.

El alquilar un vehículo en Zimbabwe puede resultar caro, así que si viaja con presupuesto limitado, es mejor formar parte de un grupo para que resulte más favorable. Además, los vehículos de alquiler son es-

casos, así que es mejor reservarlos con bastante anticipación.

Botswana Para disfrutar al máximo de Botswana se necesita un vehículo o se debe disponer de mucho tiempo y paciencia para 'ir echando dedo'. Los viajes por carretera en Botswana se pueden clasificar dentro de una de las tres categorías siguientes: un viaje de prisa a gran velocidad, a través de las excelentes carreteras asfaltadas; un incierto movimiento por las pobres carreteras secundarias o una expedición a través de los terrenos más salvajes en un vehículo de pasajeros de chasis alto con transmisión en las cuatro ruedas o en un camión.

Las motocicletas convencionales rinden bien en las carreteras asfaltadas y las motocicletas de alta potencia pueden brindar mucha diversión en las vías desérticas, pero hay carreteras donde las nubes de polvo y la arena lanzada por los vehículos de alta velocidad convertirán el viaje en motocicleta en una experiencia muy desagrable. Hay que recordar que no se admiten motocicletas en los parques nacionales ni en las reservas.

Las carreteras secundarias de Botswana consisten en un laberinto de senderos surcados y caminos rurales que se cruzan y que pueden completamente confundir a los conductores de

ALEX DISSANAYAKE

Lion, Hwange National Park, Zimbabwe

vehículos. Aún más, muy pocos de estos caminos rurales aparecen en los mapas y muchos de estos son rutas creadas de manera espontánea y sostenidos solamente por el uso. Cuando están demasiado surcados, inundados o con demasiado lodo para transitarlos, una nueva ruta es creada. Indicativo de las condiciones cambiantes de la superficie son las múltiples sendas paralelas que se separan y se unen otra vez, se cruzan, se desvían y regresan de nuevo, y hasta desaparecen completamente en algunas ocasiones.

El alquilar un vehículo, especialmente uno de transmisión en las cuatro ruedas, requiere disponer de una buena cantidad de dinero, pero brindará la oportunidad de pasear libremente y explorar lo mejor que puede ofrecer el país. Mejor aún, permitirá visitar el desierto Kalahari, que es una de las áreas silvestres más pristinas del Africa.

Namibia Hasta ahora, la manera más fácil de movilizarse alrededor de Namibia es por carretera. Un excelente sistema de carreteras asfaltadas recorre totalmente el país desde la frontera sud africana en Nakop y Noordoewer hasta Divundu al noreste y Ruacana al noroeste.

De manera similar, carreteras secundarias asfaltadas conectan las arterias principales de norte a sur con Gobabis, Lüderitz, Swakopmund y la Bahía Walbis. A lo largo del resto del país, la mayoría de los pueblos y parajes están conectados por buenas rutas de grava. Como regla general, las autopistas marcadas con las letras B y C están bien cuidadas y son pasables por todos los vehículos. Las marcadas con la letra D pueden ser un poco más rugosas pero, a menudo, son pasables por vehículos de transmisión en dos ruedas. Sin embargo, el conducir en las car-

reteras de grava puede ser, en el mejor de los casos, dificultoso, y en el peor, traicionero – ¡hay que tener cuidado! Debe recordarse que no se permiten las motocicletas en ningún parque nacional, excepto en las rutas principales a través del parque Namib-Naukluft.

El alquiler de vehículos es caro, pero en grupo, es la manera mejor y más directa de ver el país. Es aconsejable reservar los vehículos con buena anticipación.

En Bicicleta

Zimbabwe Las rutas principales de Zimbabwe son revestidas y en condición excelente, y los bordes de las vías a menudo están asfaltadas y separados del tráfico principal por medio de líneas amarillas pintadas, de tal manera que pueden usarse como vías para bicicletas. Sin embargo, es importante tener en cuenta que no se admiten las bicicletas en los parques de animales.

Las piezas de recambio son muy escasas, aún en Harare, así que se deben traer todas las herramientas y los recambios que uno crea que pueda necesitar.

Botswana Es en general plano, pero esta es la única ventaja que le ofrece a los ciclistas. A menos que se sepa lo que se está haciendo, se debe abandonar cualquier idea que se tenga de aventurarse en Botswana en bicicleta. Las distancias son enormes; los horizontes son vastos; el clima y el panorama son tórridos y secos; el sol es intenso, a través del aire claro y semitropical del desierto; y aún a lo largo de las vías principales, el agua es escasa y los pueblecillos esparcidos a grandes distancias.

En las carreteras, rectas y asfaltadas, el límite de velocidad nacional de 110 km por hora no impide que éste se sobrepase, y cuando un semirremolque pasa a 150 km por hora, los ciclistas pueden ser lanzados inadver-

tidamente fuera de la vía por la fuerza del viento producido. Las bicicletas también son inadecuadas para lograr acceso a las zonas alejadas a las vías – incluso los ciclistas más experimentados han declarado que la mayoría de las vías del país son imposibles para las bicicletas. A lo largo de las carreteras sin asfalto, los vehículos chillan al pasar levantando nubes de arena y polvo, y en las rutas menos utilizadas es probable enfrentarse a profundas arenas movedizas. A menos que se esté dispuesto a llevar cargados el equipaje y la bicicleta a través de largas e inhabitadas distancias, no se debe aventurar a salir de las rutas principales. También hay que tener en cuenta que las bicicletas no son permitidas en las reservas fauna silvestre en Botswana.

Namibia En cuanto al terreno, los espacios ampliamente abiertos de Namibia son generalmente amenos para los ciclistas, pero hay que recordar que las distancias entre los pueblecillos son vastas y el agua es generalmente escasa, así que se deben llevar reservas abundantes. Además, las condiciones climáticas pueden ser penosas, desde calores intensos y secos hasta el intenso viento con neblina pesada o arena llevada por el viento. De nuevo, las bicicletas no son permitidas dentro de los parques nacionales ni en las reservas de fauna silvestre.

En Bote

Zimbabwe Puesto que Zimbabwe es un país sin salida al mar, los únicos botes dignos de tenerse en cuenta son los dos sistemas de transbordadores que operan en el Lago Kariba entre la población de Kariba y Binga o Mlibizi cerca a lado oeste del lago. Estos son útiles especialmente si se quiere hacer un tur circular de Zimbabwe sin volver para atrás, entre las Cataratas Victoria y Bulawayo.

ジンバブエ、ボツワナ、ナミビアの旅

バス

ジンバブエ

ジンバブエには急行とローカルの二種類のバスがある。急行バスは比較的能率よく時刻表通りに運行している。ローカルバスは国内のほぼすべての地域に行き、急行バスと同じくらい速いこともあるが、サービスと正確さはまちまちだ。

ローカルバスは混むことがあるが格安だ。外国人旅行者が主に利用する急行バスを使うより、ローカルバスを利用した方がジンバブエの人々と接することができる。主要都市を結ぶ路線は、バスが満員になり次第一日中発車しているが、いなかに行く時は、遅くとも午前六時にはバス停に行く必要がある。

ほとんどのローカルバスは、ムシカ（mushika）またはレンキニ（renkini）— 街の郊外にある市場 — から発車する。大きい市や町には『市内バスターミナル』もある。

ボツワナ

ボツワナの公共道路交通網は大変乏しい。バスとミニバスは、主に東部を運行している。運行スケジュールは変わりやすく、バスは普通、満員になるまで発車しない。だから朝早く出発場所に行くのが最良だ。バス旅行は時間がかかる。特にロバツェ（Lobatse）とフランシスタウン（Francistown）を結ぶルートではヒッチハイクや、または、遅いが時間通りに運行する電車で旅行する人が多い。

ナミビア

ナミビアのバスの交通網はあまり発達していない。デラックス・バスはウィンドーク（Windhoek）、ケープタウン（Cape Town）、ヨハネスブルグ（Johannesburg）を結ぶ便と、スバコプムンド（Swakopmund）、ウォルビス・ベイ（Walvis Bay）、ツメブ（Tsumeb）を結ぶいくつかの便に限られている。

ローカルのミニバスがB1号線（国を南北に結ぶ幹線道路）を往復しており、ウィンドーク（Windhoek）を中心に、北はオシャカティ（Oshakati）、南はキートマンショープ（Keetmanshoop）まで運行している。

電車

ジンバブエ

ジンバブエにはよく発達した鉄道網があり、ハラーレ（Harare）、ブラワーヨ（Bulawayo）、ビクトリア滝（Victoria Falls）、ムタレ（Mutare）などの大都市を結んでいる。運賃はとても安く、三等席、エコノミー・クラスは特に安い。これらの席は急行以外のすべての便にある。

ジンバブエの電車はほとんどが夜行で、また、比較的走行距離が短いため、翌朝、都合の良い時間帯に目的地に到着するように、ゆっくりと走行する。寝台室、寝具は安く、キャンプ旅行をしてい

DEANNA SWANEY

Sand dunes, Namib Desert, Namibia

る場合は特にゆっくりと休める。

　普通、客室は男女別になっているが追加料金を払えば家族用または二人用の客室（coupé）を予約できる。国際電車の場合、飲食料金は通過中の国の通貨で支払わなくてはいけない。車掌が鍵を管理している二人用客室（coupé）以外、客室を出る時は必ずだれかに荷物をみてもらうか自分で持って行くこと。

　国内、国際電車とも、できるだけ早く席を予約することを勧める。

ボツワナ

だだっ広くてほこりっぽい、ほとんど見所がないボツワナの荒野を通過するには、スピードは遅いけれども、電車を使うとリラックスできる。鉄道はジンバブエ国境のラモグェバーナ（Ramokgwebana）から、南アフリカ共和国国境のラトラバーマ（Ramatlhabama）までとおっているが、現在、南はロバツェ（Lobatse）までしか運行していない。主な停車駅は、ハボローネ（Gaborone）、マハラピエ（Mahalapye）、パラピエ（Palapye）、セルーレ（Serule）、フランシスタウン（Francistown）。ハボローネ（Gaborone）、ロバツェ（Lobatse）間は通勤電車も運行している。

ナミビア

主な都市を結ぶ鉄道網は比較的発達しているが、電車はとても遅い。ある読者は「ちょっと元気のあるロバが引く荷車のペースだ」と表現した。さらに、一本の列車に客車と貨物車が混ざっているので、すべての駅に停車することもよくある。

　一方、鉄道はあまり人気がある旅行手段ではないので、予約で満席になることはほとんどない。すべての電車にエコノミークラス

と寝台席がある。客室一つ当り寝台が４つまたは６つあるが、格安の三等車両には座席だけがある。寝台席が欲しい場合はあらかじめ予約をしておくこと。予約がないと一等車両に入れられることがある。

道路

ジンバブエ

自家用車を使えば、どこでも止まることができ、国立公園にも気軽に行け、公共交通機関が通っていないところでも行くことができる。ジンバブエの広い高速道路では、オートバイも十分使えるが、国立公園内の乗り入れは禁止されている。

　国外で登録した車は無料で一時輸入できる。保険に加入していない時は、料金は高いが入国時に第三者賠償保険に入ることができる。また、レンタカーをボツワナ、ナミビア、南アフリカ共和国から持ち込むこともできる。

　ジンバブエでは、母国からの運転免許証が英語ならば９０日間まで通用する。英語でない場合は、認定された英語訳と、本人の写真が必要。ジンバブエのレンタカーは高いので安くあげたい時は数人のグループで借りることを勧める。なお、レンタカーの台数が少ないのでできるだけ早く予約すること。

ボツワナ

ボツワナを楽しみたい時は、車を使うか、またはヒッチハイクのためのたっぷりな時間、忍耐力が必要だ。道路を使ってボツワナを旅行する場合はつぎの三種類の体験をすることができる。第一に舗装道路網を使って迅速に移動すること。第二に何が起こるか予測できない二級道路をゆっくり走ること。第三に車高が高くて丈夫な四輪駆動やトラックで、人の通らない土地を探検すること。普通のオートバイは舗装道路を旅行するには便

利だ。また、強力なモトクロス仕様のオートバイで砂漠を突き抜けるのは楽しい。しかし、二級道路では高速で走る他の車のほこりと砂でひどい体験をする。国立公園と保護地区ではオートバイの乗り入れは禁止されているので注意すること。

　ボツワナの裏道は、ウサギの巣やけもの道が多く、迷路のようになっていて迷いやすい。その上、これらの道は地図に載っていない場合が多く、臨時的にできたものが多い。穴ででこぼこになったり、洪水で流されたり、泥沼状態になったりすると新しい道ができる。このような道の分かれ具合で土地の状態の変化が良く分かる。

　レンタカー、特に四輪駆動の車を借りるにはかなりの出費を覚悟すること。しかし、車を使えば自由に探検でき、この国の特徴が良くわかる。とくにアフリカで一番原始的な地域のひとつ、カラハリ砂漠に行くことも可能になる。

ナミビア

ナミビアを旅するのに一番楽な方法は道路を使うことだ。舗装道路網はよく発達していて、南アフリカ共和国国境のナコプ（Nakop）とノルドヴェル（Noordoewer）から、北東にあるディブンドゥ（Divundu）と北西にあるルアカナ（Ruacana）までつながっている。

　舗装道路は、南北を貫く幹線から枝分かれしていて、ゴバビス（Gobabis）、リュデリッツ（Lüderitz）、スバコプムンド（Swakopmund）、ウォルビス・ベイ（Walvis Bay）を結んでいる。それ以外の町は良く整備されている砂利道でつながっている。基本的にBとCの記号が付く国道は良く整備されていてどんな車でも通行できる。Dの記号がつく道は多少揺れるが四輪駆動の車でなくても通れることが多い。しかし、砂

利道を運転するには危険を伴うので技術が必要だ。十分注意すること。

ナミブ・ナウクロフト公園（Namib-Naukluft park）を通る幹線道以外すべての国立公園にオートバイで立ち入る事は禁止されている。レンタカーは高いが数人で借りれば一番楽に旅をすることができる。車の予約はできるだけ早い時期にした方がいい。

自転車
ジンバブエ

ジンバブエの幹線道路はすべて舗装されていてよく整備されている。路肩も舗装してあり、黄色い線で車線と区別してあるのでこの部分を自転車用に使うことができる。自転車の部品はハレーレ（Harare）でも購入できないので必要な道具や部品は持参すること。

ボツワナ

ボツワナはサイクリストにとって、平坦だという点以外に良いことはない。経験がない場合、ボツワナを自転車旅行することは避けた方がいい。長距離でだだっ広いだけだ。この地域は亜熱帯砂漠地域なので、日光が強く乾燥している、幹線道路沿いでも水が少なく、村から村の距離が長い。平坦でまっすぐな舗装道路は最高速度は110キロだが、制限速度を越えてとばす車が多い。セミトレーラーが150キロでそばを通り抜ける時は、サイクリストが風圧で吹き飛ばされる時もある。裏道を通るにも自転車は適切ではない。経験をつんだサイクリストもほとんどの道は無理だという。未舗装の道では車が通り抜ける時ほこりと砂を巻き上げる。また、あまり使用されていない道には砂の吹き溜りがある。自分で自転車と荷物を長距離運ぶ準備がないときは幹線道路から離れないほうが無難だ。ボツワナの動物保護地域は自転車の立入が禁止されている。

ナミビア

地形からすると、ナミビアの広大な土地はサイクリストにとっては旅行しやすいといえる。しかし、村と村との距離はとても長く、水が少ないので、物資を十分補給できるよう準備しておくことを忘れずに。また、天候は厳しく、乾燥した猛暑や強風をともなう濃霧や砂嵐など様々だ。国立公園と動物保護地域への自転車の乗り入れは禁止されている。

ボート
ジンバブエ

ジンバブエは陸に囲まれた国なのでカリバ湖（Lake Kariba）のカリバ町（Kariba town）と湖の西端のビンガ（Binga）、またはムリビジ（Mlibizi）をつなぐ二航路のフェリーしかない。ビクトリア滝（Victoria Falls）、ブラワヨ（Bulawayo）間を引き返さずにジンバブエを回遊したい時は便利だ。

PETER PTSCHELINZEW

CHRIS BARTON

DAVID WALL

Top: White Rhinoceros, Zimbabwe
Bottom: Elephants, Etosha National Park, Namibia
Right: Giraffe, Okavango Delta, Botswana

Index

Kildonan (Zim) 18 D3
King Mine (Zim) 26 D2
Kinross (RSA) 33 G6
Klein Aub (Nam) 29 E2
Klein Nauas (Nam) 29 G1
Kleinsee (RSA) 34 D5
Klerksdorp (RSA) 32 D6
Klipdam (Nam) 35 H1
Klipneus (Nam) 28 C1
Kliprand (RSA) 35 F6
Kobos (Nam) 29 F2
Kodibeleng (Bot) 25 F6
Koedoeskop (RSA) 33 E4
Kokerboomwoud (Nam) 29 H6
Kokong (Bot) 31 G3
Kombat (Nam) 22 B1
Kongola (Nam) 16 B4
Koranderkolk (RSA) 35 H5
Korodziba (Zim) 25 G1
Kos (Nam) 29 E1
Koster (RSA) 32 D5
Kotwa (Zim) 19 G3
Kotzehoop (RSA) 35 E4
Kousant (RSA) 30 C4
Kowares (Nam) 13 E6
Kowas (Nam) 22 B6
Koës (Nam) 30 A5
Krasbrak (RSA) 30 C5
Kronendel (Nam) 13 F6
Krugersdorp (RSA) 33 F5
Kubis North (Nam) 29 H6
Kudumatse (Bot) 33 E1
Kuis (Nam) 29 G2
Kuke (Bot) 23 H3
Kule (Bot) 23 E6
Kumuchuru (Bot) 24 B5
Kurai (Zim) 27 F1
Kwadiba (Bot) 25 F3
Kwang (RSA) 30 C4
Kwaviyi (Nam) 15 G5
Kwe Kwe (Zim) 18 C6
Kwenda (Zim) 19 F6

Labora (Nam) 22 D4
Laersdrif (RSA) 33 H4
Lalapanzi (Zim) 18 D6
Lancaster (Zim) 26 B2
Langklass (RSA) 30 C4
Langklip (RSA) 35 H3
Lead Mine (RSA) 32 D5
Lebowakgomo (RSA) 33 H3
Leeupoort (RSA) 33 E4
Legion Mine (Zim) 26 A4
Legkraal (RSA) 33 H1
Lehututu (Bot) 31 E2
Lekkersing (RSA) 34 D4
Lekkerwater (RSA) 30 C4
Lendepas (Nam) 30 B3
Lentsweletau (Bot) 32 C3
Leonardville (Nam) 29 H1
Lephephe (Bot) 32 C1
Lerala (Bot) 25 H6
Lethakane (Bot) 25 E4
Letlhakeng (Bot) 32 B2
Lichtenburg (RSA) 32 C5
Lichtenfels (Nam) 29 G5
Limburg (RSA) 33 G2
Lindfontein (Nam) 29 H2
Lindleyspoort (RSA) 32 D4
Linyanti (Nam) 16 C4
Lions Den (Zim) 18 D3
Livingstone (Zam) 17 E4
Lobatse (Bot) 32 C4
Lochinvar (Zim) 19 E4
Lokalane (Bot) 23 H6
Lokwabe (Bot) 31 E2
Lonely Mine (Zim) 26 B1
Lose (Bot) 25 G6

Lothian (Zim) 27 E2
Lotlhakane (Bot) 32 B4
Louis Trichardt (RSA) 26 C6
Louwatersuid (Nam) 29 G1
Lua (Ang) 12 D1
Luano (Ang) 13 E2
Lubimbi (Zim) 17 G5
Lüderitz (Nam) 28 D6
Luengue (Ang) 15 E2
Luhebu (Nam) 23 E1
Luiana (Ang) 16 B3
Lukampa (Zim) 18 B6
Lupala (Nam) 14 D4
Lupane (Zim) 17 H6
Lusaka (Zam) 18 A1
Lusitu (Zam) 18 B1
Lusulu (Zim) 17 H4

Maamba (Zam) 17 G3
Maanhaarrand (RSA) 33 E5
Maasstroom (RSA) 26 A6
Mabalabuta (Zim) 27 F5
Mabeleapudi (Bot) 25 G5
Mabeskraal (RSA) 32 D4
Mabilaito (Ang) 12 D2
Mabiriya (Zim) 25 G1
Maboleni (Zim) 18 C6
Mabopane (RSA) 33 F5
Mabula (RSA) 33 F3
Mabule (Bot) 31 H5
Mabutsane (Bot) 31 G3
Macai (Ang) 14 D3
Machachuta (Zim) 26 C5
Machaila (Moz) 27 H5
Machaneng (Bot) 33 E1
Macheke (Zim) 19 F4
Machihiri (Zim) 18 B3
Machipanda (Moz) 19 G6
Maçobere (Moz) 27 G3
Madaba (Zim) 25 H3
Madadzi (Zim) 18 C3
Madhlambudzi (Zim) 25 H2
Madiakgama (RSA) 31 H5
Madikwe (RSA) 32 D4
Madziba (Zim) 25 H1
Madzilobge (Bot) 25 H4
Madziwa Mine (Zim) 19 F3
Madziwadzido (Zim) 18 A4
Mafikeng (RSA) 32 C5
Mafungo (Bot) 25 G3
Magaliesburg (RSA) 33 E5
Magunge (Zim) 18 C3
Mahalapye (Bot) 25 G6
Mahetlwe (Bot) 32 C3
Mahusekwa (Zim) 19 E5
Máigoé (Moz) 19 F1
Main Camp (Zim) 17 G5
Maitengwe (Bot) 25 G2
Majwaneng (Bot) 25 H6
Makado (Zim) 26 C4
Makaha (Zim) 19 G3
Makalamabedi (Bot) 24 C2
Makaleng (Bot) 25 G3
Makapaanstad (RSA) 33 F4
Makoli (Zam) 17 F4
Makopong (Bot) 31 F4
Makori Range (Zim) 19 E3
Makosa (Zim) 19 G3
Makose (Zim) 19 G3
Makumbi (Zim) 19 E3
Makunda (Bot) 23 E5
Makuti (Zim) 18 B2
Makwate (Bot) 33 E1
Makwiro (Zim) 18 D4
Malabas (Zim) 26 A4
Malaita (RSA) 33 H4
Malaka (Bot) 25 G6
Malapati (Zim) 27 E5

Maleoskop (RSA) 33 H4
Maleshe (Bot) 31 F5
Malimasindi (Zim) 18 A5
Malolwane (Bot) 32 D3
Malopowabojang (Bot) 32 C4
Malotwana (Bot) 32 C3
Maltahöhe (Nam) 29 F3
Malube (Zim) 18 D5
Mambeco (Moz) 27 H6
Mambova (Nam) 16 D4
Mamuno (Bot) 23 E5
Manaculama (Ang) 12 C3
Mandamabwe (Zim) 26 D2
Mandié (Moz) 19 H2
Mangetti (Nam) 14 C5
Mangwe (Zim) 25 H3
Mangwendi (Zim) 19 E5
Manica (Moz) 19 H6
Manjolo (Zim) 17 G4
Mankgodi (Bot) 32 A3
Manyana (Bot) 32 C3
Manywe (Zim) 18 D5
Maokane (Bot) 32 A4
Maope (Bot) 25 G6
Mapai (Moz) 27 F6
Maphashalala (Bot) 32 D2
Maphisa (Zim) 26 A3
Mara (RSA) 26 C6
Marble Hall (RSA) 33 H4
Marie se Draai (Bot) 30 C4
Mariental (Nam) 29 G3
Marikana (RSA) 33 E5
Marnitz (RSA) 33 F1
Maroelaboom (Nam) 14 C6
Marondera (Zim) 19 F5
Marongora (Zim) 18 B2
Martin's Drift (RSA) 25 H6
Marula (Zim) 25 H2
Maruleng (Bot) 25 E4
Maryland (Zim) 18 D4
Masama (Bot) 32 D2
Mashari (Nam) 15 E4
Mashava (Zim) 26 D2
Mashito (Bot) 23 G1
Masole (Zim) 26 C5
Masope (Bot) 32 A2
Massala (Moz) 19 F1
Massangena (Moz) 27 H4
Massucalane (Moz) 27 G6
Masunga (Bot) 25 H3
Masvingo (Zim) 27 E2
Mata Mata (RSA) 30 B5
Mataga (Zim) 26 D3
Mate (Nam) 16 C4
Matemo (Ang) 12 D2
Matende (Ang) 14 C3
Matetsi Headquarters (Zim) 17 H5
Mathambgane (Bot) 25 G3
Mathathane (Bot) 26 B5
Matima (Bot) 24 C2
Matlabas (RSA) 33 E3
Matlapaneng (Bot) 24 B2
Matlope (Bot) 25 H6
Matopos (Zim) 26 A2
Matrooster (RSA) 32 D4
Matsitama (Bot) 25 G3
Maué (Ang) 14 D3
Maun (Bot) 24 B2
Maunatlala (Bot) 25 H6
Mavele (Ang) 13 E2
Mavengue (Ang) 14 D3
Mavinga (Ang) 15 E1
Mavita (Moz) 27 H1
Mávue (Moz) 27 G4
Mawana (Bot) 15 H5
Mayoba (Zam) 17 F3
Mazabuka (Zam) 17 H1
Mazowe (Zim) 19 E3

Mazunga (Zim) 26 C4
Mazói (Moz) 19 H2
Mbalabala (Zim) 26 B2
Mbamba (Zim) 25 H2
Mberengwa (Zim) 26 C2
Mbizi (Zim) 27 E4
Mboane (Bot) 32 A2
McCarthysrus (RSA) 31 F5
Melfort (Zim) 19 E4
Melkviel (RSA) 30 D5
Melumba (Ang) 13 H3
Melunga (Ang) 13 F3
Melunga (Ang) 13 H3
Menatshe (Bot) 24 C6
Mengwe (Bot) 25 G2
Merindol (RSA) 33 E5
Mermaids Pool (Zim) 19 E4
Messina (RSA) 26 D5
Messum Crater (Nam) 21 E4
Metlobo (Bot) 32 B4
Mhangura (Zim) 18 D3
Mica (Ang) 14 D4
Middelburg (RSA) 33 H5
Middelpos (Nam) 29 E3
Middlepits (RSA) 31 E6
Millvale (RSA) 32 D5
Mingoje (Ang) 14 C3
Missa de Mongua (Ang) 13 F3
Mkubazi (Zim) 25 H1
Mkwasine (Zim) 27 F3
Mlibizi (Zim) 17 G4
Mmabatho (RSA) 32 C5
Mmadinare (Bot) 25 H5
Mmalogong (Bot) 30 D6
Mmamabula (Bot) 32 D1
Mmankgodi (Bot) 32 A3
Mmashoro (Bot) 25 F5
Mmathethe (Bot) 32 B4
Mmatshumo (Bot) 25 E3
Mochudi (Bot) 32 C3
Mogalakwenastroom (RSA) 33 G2
Mogapi (Bot) 25 H5
Mogapinyana (Bot) 25 H5
Mogoditshane (Bot) 32 C3
Mogojwagojwe (Bot) 32 B4
Mogonye (Bot) 32 C3
Mogorosi (Bot) 25 F5
Mohembo (Bot) 15 G5
Moimba (Ang) 12 C2
Moiyabana (Bot) 25 F6
Mokamole (RSA) 33 G2
Mokgomane (Bot) 32 B5
Mokobeng (Bot) 25 H6
Mokuti (Nam) 14 A6
Molalatau (Bot) 26 A5
Molapo (Bot) 24 C4
Molatswane (Bot) 23 H2
Molepolole (Bot) 32 C3
Mon Desir (Nam) 13 F6
Monarch (Bot) 25 H3
Mongua (Ang) 13 F2
Monsterius (RSA) 33 H4
Monte Christo (RSA) 33 E1
Montrose (RSA) 30 C5
Monze (Zam) 17 H2
Mooifontein (Nam) 29 F5
Mooifontein (RSA) 32 B5
Mookane (Bot) 32 D2
Mopane (RSA) 26 C6
Mopipi (Bot) 24 D4
Moravet (RSA) 30 C5
Moremaoto (Bot) 24 C2
Morgenzon (RSA) 33 H6
Moroka (RSA) 25 H2
Morokweng (RSA) 31 G5
Mosetse (Bot) 25 G3
Moshaneng (Bot) 32 B4
Mosita (RSA) 32 A5

Rakops (Bot) 24 C3
Ramatlhabama (Bot) 32 C5
Ramokgonani (Bot) 25 H6
Ramokgwebana (Bot) 25 H3
Ramotswa (Bot) 32 C3
Ranaka (Bot) 32 B4
Randburg (RSA) 33 F5
Rankin's Pass (RSA) 33 F3
Rasesa (Bot) 32 C3
Ratombo (RSA) 26 D6
Redcliff (Zim) 18 C6
Rehoboth (Nam) 29 F1
Renco (Zim) 27 E2
Rex (RSA) 33 E5
Riekertsdam (RSA) 32 D4
Rietfontein (Nam) 22 B1
Rietfontein (Nam) 23 F5
Rietfontein (RSA) 30 C6
Rietkolk (RSA) 33 H2
Rietoog (Nam) 29 E2
Rito (Ang) 14 D2
Rivungo (Ang) 15 H2
Rocky Spruit (Zim) 19 E5
Rodean (Nam) 21 E1
Roedtan (RSA) 33 G3
Rooibank (Nam) 28 C1
Rooiberg (RSA) 33 E3
Rooibokkraal (RSA) 32 D2
Rooibosbult (RSA) 33 E2
Rooigrond (RSA) 32 C5
Rooikop (Nam) 21 E6
Rooikop (RSA) 30 C4
Rooikraal (RSA) 33 H4
Rooiputs (RSA) 30 C5
Roolbrak (RSA) 30 C5
Roossenekal (RSA) 33 H4
Rosh Pinah (Nam) 34 D2
Rotanda (Moz) 27 H1
Rotunda (Ang) 13 E2
Ruacana (Nam) 14 E3
Ruimte (Nam) 23 E6
Rukomechi (Zim) 18 C2
Rundu (Nam) 14 D4
Rupisi (Zim) 27 G2
Rusape (Zim) 19 F5
Rushinga (Zim) 19 G2
Rustenburg (RSA) 33 E5
Rutenga (Zim) 27 E4
Ruwa (Zim) 19 E4

Sablevale (Zim) 26 B3
Sadza (Zim) 19 E6
Safari Crossroads (Zim) 17 G5
Salajwe (Bot) 32 A2
Salem (Nam) 22 D1
Salonga (Ang) 14 A1
Sambusu (Nam) 14 D4
Samugalengue (Ang) 14 D3
Sandton (RSA) 33 F5
Sandawana Mine (Zim) 26 C3
Sandála (Ang) 14 C3
Sangoshe (Bot) 15 H5
Sangwali (Nam) 16 B5
Sanitatis (Nam) 12 C5
Sannieshof (RSA) 32 C6
Santa Clara (Ang) 13 G3
Santidkwe (Bot) 24 C5
Sanyatwe (Zim) 19 G5
Sao Jorge de Limpopo (Moz) 27 F6
Satena (Ang) 12 D1
Savate (Ang) 14 B3
Savuti (Bot) 16 C5
Schlip (Nam) 29 F2
Schuckmannsburg (Nam) 16 D4
Sebina (Bot) 25 G3
Sebutu (Bot) 17 E5
Seeheim (Nam) 29 G6
Seeis (Nam) 22 B5

Sefare (Bot) 25 H6
Sefophe (Bot) 25 H5
Sehithwa (Bot) 24 A2
Sekoma (Bot) 31 H3
Selebi-Phikwe (Bot) 25 H5
Seleka (Bot) 25 H6
Selous (Zim) 18 D4
Semolale (Bot) 26 B4
Semowane (Bot) 25 F2
Senanga (Zam) 16 B1
Selingsdrif (Nam) 34 D3
Senete (Bot) 25 G2
Sengwe (Zim) 27 E5
Senkobo (Zam) 17 E4
Senlac (RSA) 31 G5
Sentrum (RSA) 33 E3
Sepupa (Bot) 15 H5
Serima Mission (Zim) 27 E1
Seringkop (RSA) 33 G5
Seronga (Bot) 15 H6
Serowe (Bot) 25 G5
Serule (Bot) 25 G5
Sesfontein (Nam) 12 D6
Sesheke (Zam) 16 C4
Sesriem (Nam) 28 D3
Sessua (Ang) 14 C4
Settlers (RSA) 33 F4
Shakawe (Bot) 15 G5
Shakwe (Bot) 25 G6
Shamva (Zim) 19 F3
Shashe (Bot) 25 H4
Shashe-Mooke (Bot) 25 H4
Sherwood (Bot) 25 H6
Shirley (Nam) 29 H5
Shorobe (Bot) 24 B1
Shoshong (Bot) 25 F6
Shurugwi (Zim) 26 D1
Siabuwa (Zim) 17 H3
Sibanyati (Zam) 17 G3
Sibasa (RSA) 26 D6
Sibinda (Nam) 16 C4
Sikaatskop (RSA) 32 D4
Sikalongo (Zam) 17 G2
Sikereti (Nam) 15 F6
Sikwane (Bot) 32 D3
Silent Valley (RSA) 32 D3
Silobela (Zim) 18 C6
Silverside Mine (Zim) 18 D3
Silverstand (Nam) 22 B5
Simwani (Zam) 17 F3
Sinamatella Camp (Zim) 17 F5
Sinazongwe (Zam) 17 H3
Sinjembela (Zam) 16 B3
Sioma (Zam) 16 B2
Sitszas (RSA) 30 C5
Siviya (Bot) 25 H3
Siyabuswa (RSA) 33 G4
Skeerpoort (RSA) 33 E5
Skuinsdrift (RSA) 32 D4
Skyline Junction (Zim) 27 G1
Slurry (RSA) 32 C5
Sneyrivier (Nam) 21 H5
Sojwe (Bot) 32 C1
Solitaire (Nam) 29 E2
Somabhula (Zim) 26 C1
Somerby (Zim) 19 E4
Songo (Moz) 19 H1
Sorris Sorris (Nam) 21 F3
Sowa (Bot) 25 F3
Spes Bona (Nam) 29 E4
Springbok (RSA) 35 E5
Springboktrek Suid (Nam) 30 A6
Springbokvlatke (Nam) 29 E4
Springbokwater (Nam) 20 D2
Springs (RSA) 33 F6
Sta. Terezinha (Ang) 13 F1
Staatsdrif (RSA) 32 D4
Stampriet (Nam) 29 H3

Standerton (RSA) 33 G6
Stapleford (Zim) 19 G5
Steilloopbrug (RSA) 33 G1
Steinfeld (Nam) 29 E4
Steinhausen (Nam) 22 B5
Steinkopf (RSA) 35 E4
Stella (RSA) 32 A6
Sterkwater (RSA) 33 G2
Stockpoort (RSA) 33 E1
Stoffberg (RSA) 33 H4
Sua Split (Bot) 25 F3
Sukses (Nam) 21 H3
Sukses (Nam) 29 E3
Sukwane (Bot) 24 C3
Summerdown (Nam) 22 C4
Sun City (RSA) 33 E4
Sungue (Moz) 27 G4
Susuwe (Nam) 16 B4
Suswe (Zim) 19 G3
Swakopmund (Nam) 21 E6
Swartruggens (RSA) 32 D5
Swartwater (RSA) 26 A6
Sybrandskraal (RSA) 33 G4

Taca (Ang) 12 D1
Takatokwane (Bot) 31 H2
Takatswaane (Bot) 23 G6
Talismanis (Nam) 23 F5
Tamasane (Bot) 25 G5
Tambor (Ang) 12 B1
Tamsu (Nam) 15 F5
Tandai (Zim) 27 G1
Tara (Zam) 17 G3
Tari Kora (Nam) 15 F6
Tati Siding (Bot) 25 H4
Tchica (Ang) 13 F2
Tchipetengo (Ang) 13 E2
Techilau (Ang) 13 F2
Techiulo (Ang) 13 F2
Temba (RSA) 33 F4
Tengwe (Zim) 18 C3
Terra Firma (RSA) 31 G5
Terrace Bay (Nam) 20 C2
Thabatshukudu (Bot) 25 E3
Thabazimbi (RSA) 33 E3
The Range (Zim) 19 E6
Thini (Bot) 25 G2
Thomson Junction (Zim) 17 F5
Thuli (Zim) 26 B5
Tlhabala (Bot) 25 F5
Tlalamabele (Bot) 25 F4
Tlokweng (Bot) 32 C3
Tlokweng Gate (Bot) 32 C3
Tobane (Bot) 25 H5
Tolwe (RSA) 26 A6
Tom Burke (RSA) 25 H6
Tombua (Ang) 12 A1
Tompi Seleka (RSA) 33 H3
Tonash (RSA) 26 B6
Tondoro (Nam) 14 C4
Tonotha (Bot) 25 H4
Toromoja (Bot) 24 D3
Torra Bay (Nam) 20 C2
Tosca (RSA) 31 H5
Toscanini (Nam) 20 D3
Toteng (Nam) 24 A2
Towla (Zim) 26 D4
Trelawney (Zim) 18 D4
Triangle (Zim) 27 F3
Tsandi (Nam) 13 F4
Tsaobis (Nam) 21 G6
Tsaraxaibis (Nam) 35 G2
Tsau (Bot) 23 H2
Tsau (Nam) 15 F5
Tsetsebjwe (Bot) 26 A5
Tsetseng (Bot) 31 G1
Tsetsserra (Moz) 19 G6

Tshabong (Bot) 31 F5
Tshane (Bot) 31 E2
Tshatswa (Bot) 30 D2
Tshawagong (Bot) 25 E3
Tshesebe (Bot) 25 H3
Tshidilamolomo (RSA) 32 A5
Tshipise (RSA) 26 D6
Tshiturapadsi (Zim) 27 E5
Tsholotsho (Zim) 25 H1
Tshootsha (Bot) 23 F5
Tshotsholo (Zim) 17 H5
Tsigara (Bot) 25 E2
Tsintsabis (Nam) 14 B6
Tsitsib (Nam) 14 C4
Tsuli (Bot) 25 F2
Tsumeb (Nam) 14 B6
Tsumkwe (Nam) 23 F1
Tswaane (Bot) 23 G5
Tuli Block Farms (Bot) 26 A6
Tunga (Ang) 14 B2
Turk Mine (Zim) 26 B1
Tutara (Nam) 21 F2
Tutume (Bot) 25 G2
Twee Rivier (Nam) 30 B4
Twee Rivieren (RSA) 30 C6
Tweeputte (Nam) 23 E2

Ugabmund (Nam) 20 D4
Uhienhorst (Nam) 29 G2
Uia (Ang) 13 E2
Uigaran (Nam) 21 F4
Uis (Nam) 21 F4
Uitoma (Ang) 13 E3
Umkando Mine (Zim) 27 G2
Umniati (Zim) 18 C5
Umsweswe (Zim) 18 C5
Union's End (Bot) 30 B3
Urikaruus (RSA) 30 C5
Us (Nam) 21 H6
Usakos (Nam) 21 G5
Uukango (Nam) 13 H4

Vaalpan (RSA) 30 C5
Vaalplass (RSA) 33 G5
Vaalwater (RSA) 33 F3
Vanalphensvlei (RSA) 33 G3
Vanderbijlpark (RSA) 33 F6
Vandyksdrift (RSA) 33 H5
Vanguard Mine (Zim) 26 C3
Vanzylsrus (RSA) 31 E6
Ventersdorp (RSA) 32 D6
Vereeniging (RSA) 33 F6
Verena (RSA) 33 G5
Vergelee (RSA) 31 H5
Verwoerdburg (RSA) 33 F5
Victoria Falls (Zim) 17 E4
Vila Nova de Vidigueira (Moz) 19 H6
Villa Nora (RSA) 33 F1
Vingerklip (Nam) 21 F2
Vioolsdrif (RSA) 35 E4
Virei (Ang) 12 C1
Vivo (RSA) 26 B6
Voigtsgrund (Nam) 29 G3
Von Lindequist Gate (Nam) 14 A6
Voorspoed (Nam) 29 E3
Vorstershoop (RSA) 31 F5
Vredeshoop (Nam) 35 G1
Vryburg (RSA) 32 A6
Vumba (Moz) 19 H6
Vuti (Zim) 18 C2

Walvis Bay (Nam) 21 E6
Warmbad (Nam) 35 F3
Warmbad (RSA) 33 F4
Warmfontein (Nam) 35 G1
Warmley (Zim) 25 H4
Warmquelle (Nam) 12 D6
Waterpoort RSA) 26 C6

Watsomba (Zim) 19 G5
Wegdraai (Nam) 30 B5
Welverdiend (Nam) 30 B5
Wenela (Nam) 16 C4
Werda (Bot) 31 G4
Wereldsend (Nam) 20 D2
Wes-Rand (RSA) 33 E5
West Nicholson (Zim) 26 C3
Wilhelmstal (Nam) 21 H5
Wilton (Zim) 19 F5
Windhoek (Nam) 22 A6
Witbank (RSA) 33 G5
Witbooisvlei (Nam) 29 H4
Witnek (RSA) 33 G4
Witpüts (Nam) 34 D2
Witvlei (Nam) 22 C5
Witvley (Nam) 29 H3
Witwater (Nam) 29 E3
Wlotzkasbaken (Nam) 21 E5
Wolwedans (Nam) 29 E4
Wonderhoek (RSA) 33 H5
Wondermere (RSA) 32 C5
Woodbine (RSA) 32 C5
Wyoming (Nam) 29 H1

Xaa (Bot) 15 H6
Xade (Bot) 24 A5
Xanagas (Bot) 23 E5
Xangongo (Ang) 13 F2
Xorodomo (Bot) 24 D4
Xumaga (Bot) 24 D2
Xumo (Bot) 24 D3

Zaka (Zim) 27 F2
Zanzibar (Bot) 26 A6
Zave (Zim) 18 D3
Zebediela (RSA) 33 G3
Zeerust (RSA) 32 C5
Zemaiwa (Zim) 18 C3
Zemalapala (Zim) 25 H1
Zhombe (Zim) 18 C6
Zikamanus (Zim) 17 H5
Zimba (Zam) 17 F3
Zoroga (Bot) 25 F2
Zumbo (Moz) 18 D1
Zvamatobwe (Zim) 19 E6
Zvishavane (Zim) 26 D2
Zwimba (Zim) 18 D4
Zwingli (RSA) 32 C3

CAMP SITES
Busi Camp (Zim) 17 H4
Deception Pan (Bot) 24 B4
Matswere Game Scout Camp (Bot)
24 C4
Mile 14 (Nam) 21 E6
Mile 72 (Nam) 21 E5
Mile 108 (Nam) 20 D4
Moreswa Pan Camp Site (Bot)
31 H1
Mucheni Camp (Zim) 17 H4
Mujima Camp (Zim) 17 H4
Nogatsaa (Bot) 16 D5
Nossob Camp (RSA) 30 C4
Okwa Camp Site (Bot) 24 B5
Piper's Pan (Bot) 24 B4
Polentswe (Bot) 30 C4
Robins Camp (Zim) 17 F5
Rooiputs (Bot) 30 D6
Sanyati West Camp (Zim) 18 B2
Sunday Pan (Bot) 24 B4
Swart Pan (Bot) 30 C3
Tashinga Camp (Zim) 18 A2
Tshinga (Bot) 16 D5
Xade Camp Site (Bot) 24 A5

CAPES & HEADLANDS
Black Cliff (Nam) 28 C2

Black Cliffs (Nam) 28 C4
Black Rock (Nam) 28 C4
Cape Cross (Nam) 20 D4
Cape Fria (Nam) 12 B5
Daiz Point (Nam) 28 D6
Dolphin Head (Nam) 28 C5
Easter Point (Nam) 28 C4
False Cape Fria (Nam) 12 B5
Hottentots Point (Nam) 28 C5
Knoll Point (Nam) 28 C4
Lüderitz Bucht (Nam) 28 D6
North Point (Nam) 28 C5
Ogden Rocks (Nam) 20 D3
Oyster Cliffs (Nam) 28 C4
Palgrave Point (Nam) 20 C2
Poacher's Point (Nam) 13 H5
Rocky Point (Nam) 12 B6
Sandveldt Tongue (Bot) 24 A1

FOREST RESERVES &
SAFARI AREAS
Charara Safari Area (Zim) 18 B2
Chesa Forest Area (Zim) 26 A2
Chete Safari Area (Zim) 17 H3
Chewore Safari Area (Zim) 18 C1
Chirinda Forest Reserve (Zim)
27 G2
Chobe Forest Reserve (Bot) 16 D5
Dande Safari Area (Zim) 18 D1
Deka Safari Area (Zim) 17 F5
Doma Safari Area (Zim) 18 D2
Gwaai Forest Land (Zim) 17 H6
Haroni-Rusitu Forest Reserve (Zim)
27 H2
Hartley Safari Area (Zim) 18 C4
Hurungwe Safari Area (Zim) 18 B1
Inseze Forest Land (Zim) 25 H1
Kasane Forest Reserve (Bot) 16 D4
Kazuma Forest Land (Zim) 17 E5
Kazuma Forest Reserve (Bot) 17 E5
Lake Alice Forest Land (Zim) 18 A6
Mafungabusi Forest Land (Zim)
18 B5
Maikaelelo Forest Reserve (Bot)
16 D5
Matetsi Safari Area (Zim) 17 E4-E5
Mtao Forest Land (Zim) 19 E6
Mzola Forest Reserve (Zim) 17 H5
Ngamo Forest Land (Zim) 17 H6
Panda-Masuie Forest Land (Zim)
17 E5
Petrified Forest (Nam) 21 E2
Sapi Safari Area (Zim) 18 C1
Sibuyu Forest Reserve (Bot) 17 E6
Sijarira Forest Area (Zim) 17 H4
Tuli Safari Area (Zim) 26 B5
Umfurudzi Safari Area (Zim) 19 F3
Vumba Forest Reserve (Zim) 19 G6

ISLANDS
Albatross Rock (Nam) 34 B1
Black Rock (Nam) 34 B2
Chief's Island (Bot) 16 A6
Halifax Island (Nam) 28 D6
Hollandsbird Island (Nam) 28 C3
Ichaboe Island (Nam) 28 C6
Kubu Island (Bot) 25 E3
Logans Island (Nam) 13 G6
Mercury Island (Nam) 28 C5
Plumpudding Island (Nam) 34 B2
Pomona Island (Nam) 34 B1
Possession Island (Nam) 34 B1
Sinclair's Island (Nam) 34 B2

MOUNTAINS & PASSES
Aha Hills (Bot) 23 F1
Ambakwe (Zim) 18 C2
Auas Mountains (Nam) 21 H6

Augub (Nam) 34 C1
Awassibberg (Nam) 28 D4
Baynes Mountains (Nam) 12 C3
Birimahwe (Zim) 18 C3
Boegoeberg (Nam) 34 C2
Bosua Pass (Nam) 21 G6
Brandberg (Nam) 21 E3
Brukkaros (Nam) 29 G5
Bungua (Zam) 18 A2
Burnt Mountain (Nam) 21 E3
Bushman Hill (Nam) 28 D4
Chidoma (Zim) 18 B2
Chinamba Hills (Bot) 16 C6
Chinyenyetsi (Zim) 18 B4
Chipitani (Zim) 18 B2
Chiribwe (Zam) 17 G3
Chironde Range (Zim) 26 D1
Chitanga (Zim) 18 C2
Chitumba (Zam) 17 G3
Chivutsisigo (Zim) 18 C2
Chouka Hills (Zim) 18 D2
Chowagasberg (Nam) 28 D4
Dundumwensi (Zam) 17 F2
East Hill (Nam) 28 C4
Ehomba (Nam) 12 D4
Ehomba Mountains (Nam) 12 D4
Erongo Mountains (Nam) 21 G4
Fletcher (Zim) 18 C3
Fransfontein Mountains (Nam)
21 F2
Gakgamala Kop (Bot) 24 B4
Garnsberg (Nam) 29 E1
Garnsberg Pass (Nam) 29 E1
Gaub Pass (Nam) 28 D1
Gcoha Hills (Bot) 16 C5
Gota Gota (Zim) 18 B2
Groot Karasberge (Nam) 35 F2
Groot Kleeberg (Nam) 22 B6
Groot Mountains (Nam) 20 D1
Groot Tirasberg (Nam) 29 E5
Grosse Münzenberg (Nam) 34 C1
Gubaatsa Hills (Bot) 16 C5
Gwiwa (Zim) 18 C3
Haina Hills (Bot) 24 B3
Hamiltonberge (Nam) 21 F6
Hanan Plateau (Nam) 29 F5
Hartman Mountains (Nam) 12 B4
Huib Hochplato (Nam) 34 D1
Huns Mountains (Nam) 34 D2
Jakkals Mountains (Nam) 34 C3
Joubert Mountains (Nam) 12 D5
Kadoma (Zim) 18 B4
Kakombo (Nam) 21 G3
Kalukumbula (Zim) 18 B2
Kalundadobola (Zam) 17 G3
Karubeamsberge (Nam) 29 G1
Kauba (Zam) 17 H3
Khomas Hochland (Nam) 21 H6
Khwebe Hills (Bot) 24 B3
Kiaora (Zim) 18 C1
Kirchberg (Nam) 28 D6
Klein Karasberge (Nam) 35 F1
Klein Spitzkoppe (Nam) 21 F5
Klinghardtsberg (Nam) 34 B1
Koubisberge (Nam) 35 E1
Kuiseb Canyon (Nam) 28 D1
Kuiseb Pass (Nam) 28 D1
Kupferberg Pass (Nam) 21 H6
Lepokole Hills (Bot) 26 A5
Longwe Range (Zam) 17 F2
Lubalansuke (Zam) 17 F2
Mababe Depresion (Bot) 16 B6
Mabeleapodi Hills (Bot) 23 H3
Mabwingombe (Zam) 17 G3
Madakwe (Zim) 18 C4
Mafungabusi Peak (Zim) 18 C5
Mafungabusi Plateau (Zim) 18 B5
Magugusi (Zim) 18 C2

Makonde (Zam) 17 E3
Makore (Zim) 18 C2
Maliko (Zam) 17 G2
Mamoluki (Bot) 25 G6
Manganyai (Zim) 18 C1
Mantowa (Zam) 17 F4
Manyame Range (Zim) 18 D3
Manyangau (Zim) 18 C2
Mapongola Hills (Zim) 18 A3
Mashava Mountains (Zim) 18 D5
Mashoro Hill (Bot) 25 F5
Masura (Bot) 25 F5
Matabe Hills (Zim) 26 C3
Mateke Hills (Zim) 27 E4
Matje M'loeji Range (Bot) 25 H4
Matuzviadonha Range (Zim) 18 B3
Mavuradonha Mountains (Zim)
19 E2-F2
Mbimbi (Zam) 18 A1
Meshwe Hill (Bot) 26 A5
Mirabib (Nam) 28 D1
Mmamanstwe Hill (Bot) 32 D3
Mokoro Hills (Bot) 25 G6
Mongwe (Zam) 17 F2
Motale (Bot) 25 F6
Mtirikati (Zim) 18 B3
Mucheka Wa-Ka Sunga Beta Moun-
tains (Zim) 18 C4
Mukajenjenje (Zam) 17 G3
Mukuruanopamaenza Hills (Zim)
19 F3
Muma (Zim) 18 B4
Munga (Zam) 17 G3
Muruazi (Zam) 17 G3
Mutimrengwa (Zim) 18 C3
Mvurvi Range (Zim) 18 D3
Mwenze (Zim) 17 G3
Mwfnezi Range 18 D5
Myove (Zim) 18 C2
Naukluft Mountains (Nam)
29 E2-E3
Ngwanalekau Hills (Bot) 24 A3
Ntaba Mangwe (Zim) 18 A4
Nurige (Zim) 18 B2
Nyanga Mountains (Zim) 19 G4
Nyangani (Zim) 19 H5
Nyongwicha (Zim) 18 B2
Okonyenya (Nam) 21 F3
Omatako (Nam) 21 H4
Otjihiba Mountains (Nam) 12 C3
Otjipateraberg (Nam) 21 F5
Owizorowe Mountains (Nam) 12 D3
Ozondjacheberg (Nam) 21 H3
Papamara (Bot) 25 F5
Paresis Mountains (Nam) 21 G2-H2
Ramara (Zim) 18 C1
Remhoogte Pass (Nam) 29 E2
Richtersveld (RSA) 34 D3
Robbies Pass (Nam) 12 D5
Rooiberg (Nam) 34 C2
Schwarze Kuppen (Nam) 12 D5
Schwarzrand (Nam) 29 F4-F5
Serorwalani (Bot) 25 F5
Sesriem Canyon (Nam) 28 D3
Shakaunda (Zam) 17 F2
Shoshong Hills (Bot) 25 F6
Shrofenstein (Nam) 35 F1
Siamonga (Zam) 17 G3
Signal Hill (Bot) 25 H4
Sijunda (Zam) 17 G3
Silvia Hill (Nam) 28 C4
Situka (Zam) 17 F4
Soutpansberg (RSA) 26 D6
Spitzkoppe (Nam) 21 F4
Spreetshoogte Pass (Nam) 29 E2
Steilrand Mountains (Nam) 12 C4
Sunday Hill (Bot) 24 C5

Ebony (Nam) 21 F5
Elephantenberg (Nam) 22 A1
Elmwood (Zim) 27 E1
Entuba (Zim) 17 F5
Epako (Nam) 21 G4
Erongo (Nam) 21 G4
Erundu (Nam) 21 H3
Etiro (Nam) 21 G4
Fairfield (Zim) 18 D6
Falkenhorst (Nam) 29 G4
Feldschuhhom (Nam) 29 G6
Felixburg Road (Zim) 27 E1
Feruka (Zim) 19 G6
Figtree (Zim) 26 A2
Francois (Nam) 21 H5
Friedrichsvelde (Nam) 21 G5
Gado (Zim) 18 C6
Gandanyemba (Zim) 27 E4
Gariganus (Nam) 29 H6
Garub (Nam) 29 E6
Garvin (Zim) 19 E3
Gawachab (Nam) 35 E1
Gebied (Nam) 29 F1
Gemsvlakte (Nam) 35 F2
Gibeon Station (Nam) 29 G4
Glassblock (Zim) 26 B3
Gobas (Nam) 29 H6
Gobo (Zim) 18 D6, 26 D1
Gorges (Nam) 35 E2
Grabwasser (Nam) 35 F2
Grand Reef (Zim) 19 G6
Grants (Zim) 25 H1
Grasplatz (Nam) 28 D6
Gresham (Zim) 18 D4
Greycourt (Zim) 18 D3
Grundomer (Nam) 29 G4
Guibes (Nam) 29 F6
Guswini (Zim) 17 H6
Gwaai (Zim) 17 H6
Haalenberg (Nam) 28 D6
Hagenau (Nam) 21 H5
Hamab (Nam) 35 G3
Hardap (Nam) 29 G3
Harmony (Zim) 26 C1
Hartseer (Nam) 21 H2
Heany Junction (Zim) 26 B2
Heide (Nam) 29 F1
Heuningberg (Nam) 21 H2
Highfields (Nam) 26 A1
Hoffnung (Nam) 22 A6
Hohental (Nam) 22 A1
Holoog (Nam) 35 E2
Houlton (Zim) 19 F4
Hunguru (Zim) 27 E1
Igusi (Zim) 25 H1, 26 A1
Indiva (Zim) 18 D6, 26 D1
Intundhla (Zim) 17 G6
Jafuta (Zim) 17 E4
Jessie (Zim) 26 B3
Jurgen (Nam) 29 G6
Kaalkop (Nam) 21 G3
Kalala (Zim) 17 E5
Kameelberg (Nam) 21 H3
Kanus (Nam) 35 F2
Kapps (Nam) 22 A6
Kashambi (Zim) 26 C2
Kasibi (Zim) 17 F5
Kennedy (Zim) 17 G6
Klein Karas (Nam) 35 E2
Kokerboom (Nam) 35 G3
Kolmanskop (Nam) 28 D6
Kombo (Zim) 26 B1
Kranzberg (Nam) 21 G5
Kums (Nam) 35 G3
Kutama (Zim) 18 D4
Leighwoods (Zim) 26 A2
Lekkerwater (Nam) 29 G2
Lembwe (Zim) 18 D3

Lesanth (Zim) 26 D4
Letshana (Bot) 25 G5
Leutwein (Nam) 22 A6
Limburgia (Zim) 27 E4
Lukosi (Zim) 17 F5
Lumane (Zim) 26 B3
Lundi (Zim) 27 E3
Lutumba (Zim) 26 D5
Luveve (Zim) 26 A2
Mabvuku (Zim) 19 E4
Madzongwe (Zim) 18 D4
Maguga (Zim) 26 B2
Makambe (Zim) 27 F4
Malindi (Zim) 17 G5
Mambanje (Zim) 17 G5
Manyame (Zim) 18 C6, 26 C1
Maope (Bot) 25 G5
Mapunga (Zim) 19 E3
Marabada (Zim) 19 G6
Marodzi (Zim) 19 E3
Martin (Zim) 18 C5
Marula (Zim) 26 A2
Masuie (Zim) 17 E4
Matamve (Zim) 26 D4
Matetsi (Zim) 17 E5
Mlagisa (Zim) 17 H6
Moreomabele (Bot) 25 G5
Mpindo (Zim) 17 H6
Msasa (Zim) 19 E4
Mtilikwe (Zim) 27 E3
Mukwakwe (Zim) 26 D2
Myrtlecham (Zim) 26 C2
Nahla (Zim) 18 C6, 26 C1
Nakop (Nam) 35 H3
Nalatale (Zim) 26 C1
Namib (Zim) 21 E6
Narib (Nam) 29 G2
Naute (Nam) 35 E1
Ngamo (Zim) 17 H6
Nonidas (Nam) 21 E6
Nora (Zim) 19 E4
Norman (Zim) 21 G4
Nossob (Nam) 22 B5
Nsiza (Zim) 26 B1
Nyombi (Zim) 27 E1
Okakombo (Nam) 21 G4
Okanono (Nam) 21 G4
Okaputa (Nam) 22 A2
Okave (Nam) 21 H5
Okazize (Nam) 21 H5
Okomukandi (Nam) 22 A2
Omatjene (Nam) 21 H2
Ondekaremba (Nam) 22 A6
Ondombo (Nam) 21 G3
Oreti (Zim) 26 D2
Orumbo (Nam) 22 B5
Osona (Nam) 21 H5
Otjihajvara (Nam) 22 A5
Otjikango (Nam) 21 H2
Otjitasu (Nam) 21 H2
Otjivero (Nam) 22 B5
Otuwe (Nam) 21 G3
Ounguati (Nam) 21 G4
Ozomba (Nam) 22 B5
Passaford (Zim) 19 E4
Ponguro (Zim) 17 F5
Pounsley (Nam) 19 G6
Quarry (Zim) 18 D6, 26 D1
Redbank (Zim) 26 A2
Rehobothstasie (Nam) 29 F1
Renders (Zim) 18 D4
Rimuka (Zim) 18 D5
Rogers (Zim) 26 B2
Rössing (Nam) 21 F6
Rotkop (Nam) 28 D6
Rusaza (Zim) 26 D3
Sabiwa (Zim) 26 B3
Salzbrunn (Nam) 29 G3

Sambawizi (Zim) 17 F5
Samwari (Zim) 18 C6
Sandown (Zim) 26 A2
Sandverhaar (Nam) 29 G6
Sango (Zim) 27 F5
Sangwe (Zim) 18 D3
Sarahuru (Zim) 26 D3
Satco (Zim) 35 F2
Sawmills (Zim) 25 H1, 26 A1
Schakalskuppe (Nam) 29 F6
Seki (Zim) 18 D4
Sekope (Zim) 18 C6, 26 C1
Selby (Zim) 19 E4
Selous (Zim) 18 D4
Shangani (Zim) 26 C1
Sherwood (Zim) 18 C5
Signalberg (Nam) 35 F2
Simplon (Nam) 29 G6
Sinkukwe (Zim) 26 B3
Stanmore (Zim) 26 B3
Stinkbank (Nam) 21 F5
Surprise (Zim) 26 C1
Syringa (Zim) 25 H2
Tafuna (Zim) 19 F3
Tarisira (Zim) 19 F5
Tatagura (Zim) 19 E3
Taupe (Bot) 25 G5
Teakland (Zim) 17 H6
Teufelsbach (Nam) 22 A5
Theydon (Zim) 19 F4
Tikwiri (Zim) 19 F5
Townlands (Nam) 29 H6
Trekkopje (Nam) 21 F5
Tsaobis (Nam) 22 A1
Tsaukaib (Nam) 29 E6
Tsawisis (Nam) 29 H5
Tsembgwe (Zim) 27 E4
Tses (Nam) 29 H5
Tshontanda (Zim) 17 F5
Tsumis Park (Nam) 29 G2
Twilight (Nam) 29 G2
Twiza (Zim) 27 F4
Tynwald (Zim) 19 E4
Umgusa (Zim) 25 H1, 26 A1
Umzibani (Zim) 25 H1, 26 A1
Unfeseri (Zim) 19 F4
Vineta (Nam) 21 E6
Vogelsang (Nam) 21 G5
Vrindskap (Nam) 21 H2
Vugwe (Zim) 26 D2
Waldau (Nam) 21 H5
Wallis (Zim) 26 D4
Wasser (Nam) 29 H5
Waterbank (Nam) 21 F5
Willoughbys (Zim) 26 C1
Wolpass (Nam) 35 G3
Wortei (Nam) 29 F1
Zaloba (Zim) 18 C6, 26 C1
Zimutu (Zim) 27 E1
Zurubi (Zim) 26 D2
Zwibale (Zim) 26 D5

RIVERS, LAKES & BAYS
Aaprivier River (Nam) 12 D6
Aba-Huab River (Nam) 21 E3
Adom River (Nam) 14 A5
Alexander River (Nam) 22 D4
Alexeck River (Nam) 22 D4
Amanzamnyama River (Zim)
 25 G1-H2
Aoub River (Nam) 29 H3, 30 C5
Babuli River (Zim) 26 A3
Bangala Dam (Zim) 27 E3
Batoka Gorge (Zim) 17 F4
Bembezi River (Zim) 18 A6
Bili River (Zim) 26 C3
Biriwiri River (Zim) 18 C3
Black-Nossob River (Nam) 22 C5

Blood River (RSA) 33 H2
Bocock's Bay (Nam) 20 D4
Boro River (Bot) 24 B1
Boteti River (Bot) 24 D3
Brak River (RSA) 26 C6
Brak River (RSA) 35 E4
Bubi River (Zim) 18 A6
Bubi River (Zim) 27 E5
Bubiana River (Zim) 26 C3
Bubye River (Zim) 26 C3
Busi River (Zim) 17 H4
Buzi River (Moz) 27 H2
Bvumvudzi River (Zim) 18 B3
Cáculuvar River (Ang) 13 E2
Cafuma River (Ang) 14 D3
Cahora Bassa Dam (Moz) 19 F1
Camchab River (Nam) 35 E3
Caquene River (Ang) 14 D4
Chamais Bay (Nam) 34 B2
Charara River (Zim) 18 B2
Chavezi River (Zim) 26 B3
Chefu River (Moz) 27 G5
Chemuumi River (Zim) 17 G6
Chezia River (Zam) 17 H2
Chikombera River (Zim) 18 B5
Chimene River (Zam) 17 G4
Chiola River (Zam) 17 H2
Chipandahouri River (Zim)18 B1
Chiredzi River (Zim) 27 F3
Chisibi River (Zam) 16 D2
Chissombo River (Ang) 14 C3
Chitake River (Zim) 18 C1
Chitolo River (Moz) 27 G5
Chobe River (Nam) 16 D4
Chora River (Zim) 18 B3
Conception Bay (Nam) 28 C2
Cuando River (Ang) 15 H2
Cuatir River (Ang) 14 B2
Cueio River (Ang) 14 B1
Cuito River (Ang) 14 D1,15 E4
Curoca River (Ang) 12 B2
Dadache River (Moz) 27 G5
Deka River (Zim) 17 F5
Dengo River (Ang) 13 H1
Devure River (Zim) 27 E1-G1
Diep River (Nam) 28 D2
Dikolaklolana River (Bot) 32 C2
Douglas Bay (Nam) 28 C6
Durissa Bay (Nam) 20 D4
Eiseb River (Nam) 22 D3, 23 E3
Ekuma River (Nam) 13 G5
Elands River (RSA) 33 G4
Elizabeth Bay (Nam) 34 B1
Epukiro River (Nam) 22 D4, 23 F3
Erundu River (Nam) 21 G2
Etaka River (Nam) 13 G4
Fish River (Nam) 29 G3, 35 E2
Fishersbrunn (Nam) 28 C3
Franciscus Bay River (Nam) 28 C4
Gachegache River (Zim) 18 B2
Gaiab River (Nam) 35 G2
Gaub River (Nam) 29 E1
Gold River (RSA) 33 F2
Goluzo River (Moz) 27 G5
Gomadommi River (Nam) 12 C5
Gomoti River (Bot) 16 B6
Great Shingwedzi River (RSA)
 27 E6
Guashigambo River (Nam) 13 G5
Gungugwe River (Zim) 18 B3
Gunib River (Nam) 22 C3
Gwaai River (Zim) 17 G5, 17 H6,
 26 A2
Gwabazabuya Stream (Zim) 25 G1
Gwampa River (Zim) 18 A6
Gwenoro Dam (Zim) 26 C1
Gweru River (Zim) 18 B6
Haib River (Nam) 35 E3

Txatora River (Moz) 19 H5
Ugab River (Nam) 20 D3, 21 F3-H2
Ume River (Zim) 18 A3-B4
Umguza River (Zim) 26 A1
Umguzama River (Zim) 25 H1
Umsangwa River (Zim) 26 B1
Umsweswe River (Zim) 18 D5
Umtshiabezi River (Zim) 26 C4
Umzingwani River (Zim) 26 B2-C4
Uniab River (Nam) 20 D2
Unkakezi River (Zim) 26 C3
Utembo River (Ang) 14 D2
Utembo River (Ang) 15 G2

Vukwe River (Bot) 25 G3
Vungu River (Zim) 18 B6
Walvis Bay (Nam) 21 E6
Washanje River (Zim) 18 C4
Wit-Nossob River (Nam) 22 C6
Xaudum River (Bot) 15 G6
Xipembe River (Moz) 27 G5
Zambezi River 16 C2-D4, 17 F4,
   18 B1, 19 H1
Zhima River (Zam) 17 G3
Zingesi River (Zim) 26 C3
Zinjo River (Zam) 17 G3
Zongwe River (Zam) 17 H3

Zoze River (Zam) 17 H3

RUINS

Bila Ruins (Zim) 26 C2
Danangombe Ruins (Zim) 26 C2
Kanye Ruins (Bot) 32 B4
Khorab Memorial (Nam) 22 A1
Nalatale Ruins (Zim) 26 C2
Nyahokwe Ruins (Zim) 19 G4
Twyfelfontein Rock Engravings
   (Nam) 21 E3
Zinjanja Ruins (Zim) 26 C2
Ziwa Ruins (Zim) 19 G4

WATERFALLS

Augrabies Falls (RSA) 35 H3
Chitove Falls (Zim) 27 G4
Epupa Falls (Nam) 12 C3
Ondorusu Falls (Nam) 12 D3
Popa Falls (Nam) 15 G5
Ruacana Falls (Nam) 13 E3
Victoria Falls (Zim) 17 E4

LONELY PLANET GUIDEBOOKS

Lonely Planet guidebooks are distributed worldwide.They are also available by mail order from Lonely Planet, so if you have difficulty finding a title please write to us. US and Canadian residents should write to Embarcadero West, 155 Filbert St, Suite 251, Oakland CA 94607, USA ; European residents should write to 10 Barley Mow Passage, Chiswick, London W4 4PH; and residents of other countries to PO Box 617, Hawthorn, Victoria 3122, Australia.

NORTH-EAST ASIA
Beijing city guide • China • Cantonese phrasebook • Mandarin Chinese phrasebook • Hong Kong, Macau & Canton • Japan • Japanese phrasebook • Korea • Korean phrasebook • Mongolia • Mongolian phrasebook • North-East Asia on a shoestring • Seoul city guide • Taiwan • Tibet • Tibet phrasebook • Tokyo city guide

INDIAN SUBCONTINENT
Bangladesh • Bengali phrasebook • India • India & Bangladesh travel atlas • Hindi/Urdu phrasebook • Trekking in the Indian Himalaya • Karakoram Highway • Kashmir, Ladakh & Zanskar • Nepal • Trekking in the Nepal Himalaya • Nepali phrasebook • Pakistan • Sri Lanka • Sri Lanka phrasebook

EUROPE
Baltic States & Kaliningrad • Baltics States phrasebook • Britain • Central Europe on a shoestring • Central Europe phrasebook • Czech & Slovak Republics • Dublin city guide • Eastern Europe on a shoestring • Eastern Europe phrasebook • Finland • France • Greece • Greek phrasebook • Hungary • Iceland, Greenland & the Faroe Islands • Ireland • Italy • Mediterranean Europe on a shoestring • Mediterranean Europe phrasebook • Poland • Prague city guide • Scandinavian & Baltic Europe on a shoestring • Scandinavian Europe phrasebook • Slovenia • Switzerland • Trekking in Greece • Trekking in Spain • USSR • Russian phrasebook • Vienna city guide • Western Europe on a shoestring • Western Europe phrasebook

NORTH AMERICA & MEXICO
Alaska • Backpacking in Alaska • Baja California • Canada • Hawaii • Honolulu city guide • Mexico • Pacific Northwest USA • Rocky Mountain States • Southwest USA • USA phrasebook

SOUTH-EAST ASIA
Bali & Lombok • Bangkok city guide • Cambodia • Indonesia • Indonesian phrasebook • Indonesian audio pack • Ho Chi Minh City guide • Jakarta city guide • Java • Laos • Lao phrasebook • Malaysia, Singapore & Brunei • Myanmar (Burma) • Burmese phrasebook • Philippines • Pilipino phrasebook • Singapore city guide • South-East Asia on a shoestring • Thailand • Thailand travel atlas • Thai phrasebook • Thai Hill Tribes phrasebook • Thai audio pack • Vietnam • Vietnamese phrasebook • Vietnamese audio pack• Vietnam travel atlas

AUSTRALIA & THE PACIFIC
Australia • Australian phrasebook • Bushwalking in Australia • Islands of Australia's Great Barrier Reef • Outback Australia • Fiji • Fijian phrasebook • Melbourne city guide • Micronesia • New Caledonia • New South Wales & the ACT • New Zealand • Tramping in New Zealand • Papua New Guinea • Bushwalking in Papua New Guinea • Papua New Guinea phrasebook • Queensland • Rarotonga & the Cook Islands • Samoa • Solomon Islands • Sydney city guide • Tahiti & French Polynesia • Tonga • Vanuatu • Victoria • Western Australia

MIDDLE EAST
Arab Gulf States • Egypt & the Sudan • Arabic (Egyptian) phrasebook • Iran • Israel • Jordan & Syria • Middle East • Turkey • Turkish phrasebook • Trekking in Turkey • Yemen

SOUTH AMERICA
Argentina, Uruguay & Paraguay • Bolivia • Brazil • Brazilian phrasebook • Chile & Easter Island • Colombia • Ecuador & the Galápagos Islands • Latin American Spanish phrasebook • Peru • Quechua phrasebook • Rio de Janeiro city guide • South America on a shoestring • Trekking in the Patagonian Andes • Venezuela

AFRICA
Africa on a shoestring • Central Africa • East Africa • Trekking in East Africa • Kenya • Swahili phrasebook • Morocco •Arabic (Moroccan) phrasebook • North Africa • South Africa, Lesotho & Swaziland • West Africa • Zimbabwe, Botswana & Namibia • Zimbabwe, Botswana & Namibia travel atlas

ISLANDS OF THE INDIAN OCEAN
Madagascar & Comoros • Maldives & Islands of the East Indian Ocean • Mauritius, Réunion & Seychelles

CENTRAL AMERICA & THE CARIBBEAN
Central America on a shoestring • Costa Rica • Eastern Caribbean • Guatemala, Belize & Yucatán: La Ruta Maya

LONELY PLANET GUIDES TO AFRICA

Africa on a shoestring
From Marrakesh to Kampala, Mozambique to Mauritania, Johannesburg to Cairo – this guidebook has all the facts on travelling in Africa. Comprehensive information on more than 50 countries.

Central Africa – a travel survival kit
This guide tells where to go to meet gorillas in the jungle, how to catch a steamer down the Congo...even the best beer to wash down grilled boa constrictor! Covers Cameroun, the Central African Republic, Chad, the Congo, Equatorial Guinea, Gabon, São Tomé & Principe, and Zaïre.

East Africa – a travel survival kit
Detailed information on Kenya, Uganda, Rwanda, Burundi, eastern Zaïre and Tanzania. The latest edition includes a 32-page full-colour Safari Guide.

Egypt & the Sudan – a travel survival kit
This guide takes you into and beyond the spectacular and mysterious pyramids, temples, tombs, monasteries, mosques and bustling main streets of Egypt and the Sudan.

Kenya – a travel survival kit
This superb guide features a 32-page Safari Guide with colour photographs, illustrations and information on East Africa's famous wildlife.

Morocco – a travel survival kit
This thoroughly revised and expanded guide is full of down-to-earth information and reliable advice for every budget. It includes a 20-page colour section on Moroccan arts and crafts and information on trekking routes in the High Atlas and Rif Mountains.

North Africa – a travel survival kit
A most detailed and comprehensive guide to the Maghreb – Morocco, Algeria, Tunisia and Libya. It points the way to fascinating bazaars, superb beaches and the vast Sahara, and is packed with reliable advice for every budget. This new guide includes a 20-page full colour section on Moroccan arts and crafts.

South Africa, Lesotho & Swaziland – a travel survival kit
Travel to southern Africa and you'll be surprised by its cultural diversity and incredible beauty. There's no better place to see Africa's amazing wildlife. All the essential travel details are included in this guide as well as information about wildlife reserves, and a 32-page full colour Safari Guide.

Trekking in East Africa
Practical, first-hand information for trekkers for a region renowned for its spectacular national parks and rewarding trekking trails. Covers treks in Kenya, Tanzania, Uganda and Malawi.

West Africa – a travel survival kit
All the necessary information for independent travel in Benin, Burkino Faso, Cape Verde, Côte d'Ivoire, The Gambia, Ghana, Guinea, Guinea-Bissau, Liberia, Mali, Mauritania, Niger, Nigeria, Senegal, Sierra Leone and Togo. Includes a colour section on local culture and birdlife.

Zimbabwe, Botswana & Namibia – a travel survival kit
Exotic wildlife, breathtaking scenery and fascinating people...this comprehensive guide shows a wilder, older side of Africa for the adventurous traveller. Includes a 32-page colour Safari Guide.

Also available:
Swahili phrasebook, Arabic (Egyptian) phrasebook & Arabic (Moroccan) phrasebook

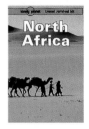

OTHER LONELY PLANET TRAVEL ATLASES

India & Bangladesh
Thailand
Vietnam

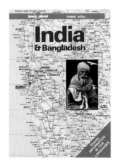

LONELY PLANET TV SERIES & VIDEOS

Lonely Planet travel guides have been brought to life on television screens around the world. Like our guides, the programmes are based on the joy of independent travel, and look honestly at some of the most exciting, picturesque and frustrating places in the world. Each show is presented by one of three travellers from Australia, England or the USA and combines an innovative mixture of video, Super-8 film, atmospheric soundscapes and original music.

Videos of each episode – containing additional footage not shown on television – are available from good book and video shops, but the availability of individual videos varies with regional screening schedules.

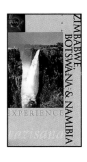

Video destinations include:

Alaska; Australia (Southeast); Brazil; Ecuador & the Galapagos Islands; Indonesia; Israel & the Sinai Desert; Japan; La Ruta Maya (Yucatan, Guatemala & Belize); Morocco; North India (Varanasi to the Himalaya); Pacific Islands; Vietnam; Zimbabwe, Botswana & Namibia.

Coming in 1996:

The Arctic (Norway & Finland); Baja California; Chile & Easter Island; China (Southeast); Costa Rica; East Africa (Tanzania & Zanzibar); Great Barrier Reef (Australia); Jamaica; Papua New Guinea; the Rockies (USA); Syria & Jordan; Turkey.

The Lonely Planet television series is produced by:
Pilot Productions
Duke of Sussex Studios,
44 Uxbridge St,
London W8 7TG, UK

Lonely Planet videos are distributed by:
IVN Communications Inc
 2246 Camino Ramon, San Ramon,
California 94583, USA

107 Power Road, Chiswick,
London W4 5PL, UK

PLANET TALK

Lonely Planet's FREE quarterly newsletter

We love hearing from you and think you'd like to hear from us.
When...is the right time to see reindeer in Finland?
Where...can you hear the best palm-wine music in Ghana?
How...do you get from Asunción to Areguá by steam train?
What...is the best way to see India?

For the answer to these and many other questions read PLANET TALK.

Every issue is packed with up-to-date travel news and advice including:

* a letter from Lonely Planet founders Tony and Maureen Wheeler
* travel diary from a Lonely Planet author – find out what it's really like out on the road
* feature article on an important and topical travel issue
* a selection of recent letters from our readers
* the latest travel news from all over the world
* details on Lonely Planet's new and forthcoming releases

To join our mailing list contact any Lonely Planet office.

Also available: Lonely Planet T-shirts. 100% heavyweight cotton (S, M, L, XL).

THE LONELY PLANET STORY

Lonely Planet published its first book in 1973 in response to the numerous 'How did you do it?' questions Maureen and Tony Wheeler were asked after driving, bussing, hitching, sailing and railing their way from England to Australia.

Written at a kitchen table and hand collated, trimmed and stapled, *Across Asia on the Cheap* became an instant local bestseller, inspiring thoughts of another book.

Eighteen months in South-East Asia resulted in their second guide, *South-East Asia on a shoestring*, which they put together in a backstreet Chinese hotel in Singapore in 1975. The 'yellow bible', as it quickly became known to backpackers around the world, soon became *the* guide to the region. It has sold well over half a million copies and is now in its 8th edition, still retaining its familiar yellow cover.

Today there are over 140 Lonely Planet titles in print – books that have that same adventurous approach to travel as those early guides; books that 'assume you know how to get your luggage off the carousel' as one reviewer put it.

Although Lonely Planet initially specialised in guides to Asia, they now cover most regions of the world, including the Pacific, South America, Africa, the Middle East and Europe. The list of *walking guides* and *phrasebooks* (for 'unusual' languages such as Quechua, Swahili, Nepali and Egyptian Arabic) is also growing rapidly.

The emphasis continues to be on travel for independent travellers. Tony and Maureen still travel for several months of each year and play an active part in the writing, updating and quality control of Lonely Planet's guides.

They have been joined by over 50 authors, 110 staff – mainly editors, cartographers & designers – at our office in Melbourne, Australia, at our US office in Oakland, California and at our European office in Paris; another five at our office in London handle sales for Britain, Europe and Africa. Travellers themselves also make a valuable contribution to the guides through the feedback we receive in thousands of letters each year.

The people at Lonely Planet strongly believe that travellers can make a positive contribution to the countries they visit, both through their appreciation of the countries' culture, wildlife and natural features, and through the money they spend. In addition, the company makes a direct contribution to the countries and regions it covers. Since 1986 a percentage of the income from each book has been donated to ventures such as famine relief in Africa; aid projects in India; agricultural projects in Central America; Greenpeace's efforts to halt French nuclear testing in the Pacific; and Amnesty International.

Lonely Planet's basic travel philosophy is summed up in Tony Wheeler's comment, 'Don't worry about whether your trip will work out. Just go!'.

LONELY PLANET PUBLICATIONS

AUSTRALIA (HEAD OFFICE)
PO Box 617, Hawthorn
3122, Victoria
tel: (03) 9819 1877
fax: (03) 9819 6459
e-mail: talk2us@lonelyplanet.com.au

USA
Embarcadero West,
155 Filbert St, Suite 251,
Oakland, CA 94607
tel: (510) 893 8555   TOLL FREE: 800 275-8555
fax: (510) 893 8563
e-mail: info@lonelyplanet.com

UK
10 Barley Mow Passage,
Chiswick, W4 4PH, London
tel: (0181) 742 3161
fax: (0181) 742 2772
e-mail: 100413.3551@compuserve.com

FRANCE
71 bis rue du Cardinal Lemoine
75005 Paris
tel: 1 46 34 00 58
fax: 1 46 34 72 55
e-mail: 100560.415@compuserve.com

World Wide Web: http://www.lonelyplanet.com/

Notes

Notes

Notes

Notes